HERBS IN THE GARDEN

Herbs in the Garden

The Art of Intermingling

ROB PROCTOR
& DAVID MACKE

INTERWEAVE PRESS

Herbs in the Garden
by Rob Proctor and David Macke

Design by Studio Signorella
Production by Dean Howes
Photography copyright ©1997 by Rob Proctor and by Joe Coca (p. 127), Dency Kane (p.56),
    Jerry Pavia (pp. 41, 93, 109, 115). Illustrations copyright ©1997 by Rob Proctor.
Text copyright ©1997 Rob Proctor and David Macke

INTERWEAVE PRESS
Interweave Press, Inc.
201 East Fourth Street
Loveland, Colorado 80537-5655

Library of Congress Cataloging-in-Publication Data
    Proctor, Rob, 1953
        Herbs in the garden: the art of intermingling / Rob Proctor
    and David Macke
            p. cm.
        Includes index.
        ISBN 1-883010-25-X
        1. Herb gardening. 2. Herbs. 3. Gardening. 4. Gardens.
        5. Gardens—Design.   I. Macke, David, 1951   .   II. Title.
        SB351.H5P76 1997
        635'.7—dc21   97–37411
                                                           CIP
Printed in Hong Kong by Sing Cheong
First Printing: 10M:1097:CC

For Mary and Arnold—thanks, folks

DESCRIPTIONS OF GARDENS INTRODUCING CHAPTERS

Introduction
Twin pastel borders of our garden lead to the folly.

Chapter 1
Rue and blue lyme grass provide a blue backdrop for variegated felicia,
Plectranthus *'Wedgwood Variegated', and thyme.*

Chapter 2
Cottage style gets a sophisticated makeover in Lauren Springer's garden with
mingled mullein, daylilies, horehound, globe thistle, and fleabane daisy.

Chapter 3
A stylish Denver border features Achillea ptarmica *'The Pearl', veronica,*
Jupiter's beard, yarrow, coneflower, and the silver spires of Artemisia *'Silver King'.*

Chapter 4
A dogwood arches over a waterlily pond as marsh marigold clings to its bank.

Chapter 5
A weathered bee skep serves as a focal point in a dry garden featuring lamb's ears.

Chapter 6
Thyme, pussytoes, and 'Pink Panda' strawberry make a utilitarian
path worth lingering over.

Chapter 7
Scented geraniums, lemon verbena, perilla, sweet potato, lotus vine,
and dusty miller create a pretty, aromatic backdoor grouping.

Reference Chart
A border of daring hues in Wheat Ridge, Colorado, glows with vivid
circle flower, prunella, geum, yarrow, and lamb's ears.

Acknowledgements

We'd like to thank the following gardeners and gardens for sharing their unique creations with us

Lauren Springer, Masonville, Colorado

Helen Dillon, Dublin, Ireland

Joanna Reed, Malvern, Pennsylvania

Sean Hogan and Parker Sanderson, Portland, Oregon

Laurie McBride, Snowmass, Colorado

Jeof Beasley and Jim Sampson, Sherwood, Oregon

Fran Davies, Aspen, Colorado

Gary Stephens, Denver, Colorado

Kathy Leishman, Vancouver, B.C.

Rosemary Verey, Barnsley, England

Lucy Hardiman, Portland, Oregon

Norma and Wayne Hazen, Wheat Ridge, Colorado

Pam Frost, Vancouver, B.C.

Yvonne England, Honeybrook, Pennsylvania

Sheila Stephens, Castle Rock, Colorado

Lorraine Higbie, Denver, Colorado

Linda Freymiller, Solano Beach, California

Bill Slater, Santa Barbara, California

Vicki Liebhaber, Santa Barbara, California

Roger Raiche, Berkeley, California

Chanticleer, Wayne, Pennsylvania

Denver Botanic Gardens, Denver, Colorado

Joy Creek Nursery, Scapoose, Oregon

North Carolina State Arboretum, Raleigh, North Carolina

University of British Columbia Botanic Gardens, Vancouver

Longwood Gardens, Kennett Square, Pennsylvania

University of California at Berkeley Botanical Gardens, Berkeley, California

Wave Hill, New York

Wisley Gardens, England

Pennsylvania Horticultural Society, Philadelphia, Pennsylvania

Hidcote Manor Garden, England

Ithaca High School, Ithaca, New York

Stourton House Garden, England

Furthermore, we acknowledge the support (moral and otherwise) from these dear people

Angela Overy, Sedalia, Colorado

Carolyn Mueller and James F. Carley, Arcada, California

Andrea McFadden and Christopher Woods, Wayne, Pennsylvania

Corinne Levy and Tom Segal, Sonoma, California

Marcia Tatroe, Aurora, Colorado

David Tarrant, Vancouver, B.C.

Diane and Tom Peace, Lockhart, Texas

Gisela Rohde, McKinleyville, California

Kim Hawkes, Chapel Hill, North Carolina

Sherill and Jim Hawkins, Glenwood Springs, Colorado

Marco Polo Stufano, New York City

Nancy Goodwin, Hillsborough, North Carolina

Panayoti Kelaidis, Denver Botanic Gardens

Betsy Gullan, Pennsylvania Horticultural Society

Susan Eubank, Helen Fowler Library, Denver Botanic Gardens

The entire staff at Interweave Press

TABLE of CONTENTS

INTRODUCTION
1 *The Making of a Garden*

CHAPTER ONE
11 *Foliage First*

CHAPTER TWO
37 *Cottage Chic*

CHAPTER THREE
49 *Boundless Borders*

CHAPTER FOUR
75 *Shade and Stream*

CHAPTER FIVE
91 *The Dryland Garden*

CHAPTER SIX
107 *Every Nook and Cranny*

CHAPTER SEVEN
119 *The Potted Herb*

REFERENCE CHART
133 *Favorite Herbs
for Intermingling*

147 *Index*

THE MAKING OF A GARDEN

WHEN WE STARTED our new garden in May 1993, we faced many decisions. One was whether to include a formal herb garden. We'd enjoyed the one at the old house, in which a series of interlocking triangular and diamond-shaped herb beds were surrounded by the vegetable garden and spanned by the grape arbors, which made the herbs a focal point. But did we really want to do that again?

Probably not. That spring we were in the mood for the new and spontaneous. Although we'd been thinking of moving for a while, and had halfheartedly looked at a few houses, we'd decided the time was not right to buy or sell. Besides, Rob was still recovering from back surgery to repair a lifetime of abuse from riding, skiing, and gardening. Then, all of a sudden, we found a wonderful old house we couldn't pass up, sold our old house, and moved—all within three weeks. That's why, in between shuttling pickup loads of boxes to the new house, we were drawing up plans for a new garden on yellow legal pads.

Most books about garden design caution the reader to wait before plunging in and digging. Stop, they say: study the lay of the land; consult the genius of the place before beginning. What genius? It was a flat lot, about an acre, in the middle of a northwest Denver neighborhood, planted in grass and a number of mature trees. To us, it was the equivalent of a blank canvas. We could not resist all the possibilities it offered.

First we hired a crew to cut down eight massive Siberian elms that had laid claim to the land many decades ago. Our new neighbors must have been horrified to watch the old giants fall, but they were in terrible shape and we didn't consider them desirable shade trees. In fact, we felt that the best way to prune those elms was right down to the base.

Next we had a dump truck deposit an enormous pile of compost in the backyard. We let the front lawn die under the baking summer sun (although one neighbor used to sneak over to sprinkle it at night because he was embarrassed). Scaffolding encircled the house as we tore down rotted molding and old gutters, and a brick cleaner tackled the grimy, century-old exterior. We carved great swaths out of the back lawn for borders and dug holes to support decorative brick columns. Our neighbor to the west spent an inordinate amount of time on his roof that summer, ostensibly adjusting his TV antenna.

A section of the pastel border is planted with pale yellow Cephalaria alpina, Digitalis lutea, *rose campion, anchusa, Armenian cranesbill, and golden hops vine.*

Our sketches served as blueprints, and we improvised as we went. The garden framework is a formal layout of borders that blends with the late-Victorian Italianate architecture of the house but provides freedom to accommodate the thousands of species of plants we grow. The notion of an all-herb garden quickly fell by the wayside. We opted for integration instead, situating plants where they were best suited and where they could make a contribution to the garden as a whole. Because different herbs have different cultural requirements, we decided to intermingle them with plants that share their needs. The culinary herbs we use most often tend to appear in areas that are just a quick dash from the kitchen or in pots on the patio, but we've discovered many other places where herbs can play a role.

Morning glories and scarlet runner beans arch over edibles and ornamentals, including strawberries, beans, poppies, and mustard.

The front garden, where our neighbors once anguished over the dead lawn, has become a planting that may be characterized as cottage style. It was inspired in part by our friend Lauren Springer's garden, in which overstuffing meets a naturalistic approach to planting. We were strongly influenced by Lauren's artistry in color and texture, and we also helped ourselves to her idea of using a flagstone path as a structural element.

We seldom water the front garden, so that's where many drought-tolerant herbs have found homes. We put others in the arid stretch of former lawn between the sidewalk and the curb that we Colorado gardeners call "hell strips". It has become a trend in the West to turn these exasperating stretches of half-dead lawn into pretty, floriferous gardens of native and adaptable plants that not only survive but prosper solely on natural rainfall. Other parts of our garden have also been designated as low-water areas where plants are grouped for conservation. In the large backyard, the plants that demand the most moisture are placed closest to the house (and the hose); plants more tolerant of drought are placed closer to the alley.

We have incorporated herbs throughout much of our garden. We try to look at each plant with an unjaded eye—ignoring how it has been used or misused in the past, then evaluating its intrinsic beauty and character and placing it where it can shine.

In our woodland and shade gardens (we didn't cut down *all* the trees), we've introduced herbs that thrive beneath protection from the fierce rays of the Mile-High-City sun. Under and around vintage maple, spruce, ash, apple, and crabapple thrive many woodland denizens that have a long history of herbal use, as well as a handful of shade-tolerant culinary favorites such as chervil and angelica. Our goldfish pond is just another excuse to grow a few aquatic herbs, while the banks of the irrigation

> We opted for integration instead, situating plants where they were best suited and where they could make a contribution to the garden as a whole.

ditch that cuts through the corner of our property allow us to grow interesting streamside and marshland herbs.

One of our trickiest experiments has been to integrate a space for vegetables into the framework of the garden. This we did by turning the traditional idea of a vegetable plot upside down. Now the vegetables and their herbal accompaniments aren't grown in rows but rather in drifts and colonies like the plants in the rest of the garden. Throughout the growing season, we enjoy bountiful crops of corn, beans, squash, and much more that are as beautiful as they are appetizing. We relish the challenge of elevating the common vegetable plot to an artistic level.

Each area of the garden presents an opportunity to show plants at their best. We use every nook and cranny, from the spaces between flagstones to the pockets between

rocks in a low retaining wall. Even a trip to the compost pile is an herbal adventure as the wheelbarrow tire releases the aroma of a few sprigs of thyme crushed beneath its tread.

We certainly don't neglect the patios. Few people are crazy enough to display 500 pots of plants each summer. We are. Our pots overflow with old favorites, culinary herbs that we snip frequently, and plants collected on travels throughout the country. They help set the stage for entertaining and relaxing outdoors.

At the rear of the property is our elevated folly (see the photo on page 1). For centuries, gardeners have been building follies—decorative outbuildings whose purpose is essentially aesthetic, whose designs are strictly at the folly of the gardener. Our folly serves several functions, but the cost of its construction—when we really should have put the money to more

We excavated a forgotten foundation, above, to create a sunken garden that supports moisture-loving woodland plants such as pulmonarias, primroses, and golden comfrey. A grouping of our nearly 500 patio pots, right, holds silver Plectranthus argentatus, *penstemons, roses, artemisia, and 'Burgundy Giant' fountain grass.*

mundane use—stamps it as True Folly, no matter what it's called.

On the other hand, who can put a price on the pleasure it brings us? The folly anchors the twin pastel borders as both focal point and destination. It provides us with shelter from the sun during breaks from gardening, and it does the same for the shade-loving houseplants that get summer vacations outdoors. A climb up the folly's spiral staircase is rewarded by a panoramic view of the garden. Here we can appreciate the

geometric outlines of the borders and the barely controlled chaos within.

ART AND SWEAT

People garden for many reasons. We're not quite sure why we do, except that we always have. We grew up gardening. If pressed, we admit that our year revolves around the garden. Some people might feel trapped by the responsibility of tending an intensively cultivated acre or the difficulty of scheduling a summer vacation, but we find the garden endlessly fascinating. It's not always a picnic—the chores are many and the hours are long—but we love the fragrant blooming space we've created.

In some ways, the garden is a giant outdoor laboratory. We experiment endlessly. Many of our plants come from seeds or cuttings that we grow in the winter basement under a tangle of fluorescent lights. We trade with friends, collect on trips, and order by mail. We've designed the garden to evolve. As we follow our collectors' instincts to acquire plants, we test them in the garden. The ones that perform best win a permanent spot and challenge us to place them gracefully within the framework.

The art of intermingling herbs invites never-ending study, and the garden is our studio. We learn from our successes, our mistakes, and from our gardening friends throughout the country. It's a wonderful

*H*ere's our definition: If you can cook with it; garnish a salad with it; soothe a burn or scratch with it; make a tea from it; soak in the tub with it; perfume your sheets with it; kill a bug with it; make a potpourri, sachet, wreath, or something good-smelling with it; treat a disease with it; weave, dye, or spin something with it; scour pots or wash with it; worm your pet with it; formulate oils and lotions to beautify your body with it; cast a spell with it; or make a big creation involving a glue gun, wheat stalks, and raffia with it—it's an herb.

*Shady contrasts include golden feverfew, wild ginger, Heuchera
'Pewter Veil', bleeding heart, cut-leaf prunella, hosta, golden moneywort,
bird's eye veronica, pulmonaria, variegated liriope, and giant cow parsnip.*

Giant sea kale, dunesilver, sea holly, garlic, and white forms of mullein and rose campion comprise a portion of our white border.

fraternity—the gardeners who practice the art and science of horticulture—and within these pages we're pleased to pass along many ideas we've learned from them, as well as photographs of their creations.

While our country is a big one, with many climates, herb gardeners have much in common. Those who have never visited Colorado may wonder what it's like to garden here—or, more likely, what relevance the experiences of two guys who garden in Denver could hold for them. Contrary to myth, we Coloradans don't all live in mountain meadows teeming with columbines among which we hand-feed the wildlife and hum John Denver songs. Most of us face the same challenges that gardeners everywhere do. It's too cold in winter and too hot in summer, it either rains too much or too lit-

tle, our soil is either too heavy or too light, and it's either too shady or too sunny for where we want to put a plant. Denver is officially designated Zone 5, but we don't pay much attention to that. The USDA zones refer only to average minimum temperatures, not to all the other conditions that help determine which plants will survive. In fact, we're in zone denial. We exploit the possibilities that exist in our climate—abundant sunshine and relatively dry winters—to expand the range of plants we can grow successfully. As a result, our palette of herbs is quite large, probably because our definition of herbs is broad. There's enough categorizing and compartmentalizing in the world. Let's skip it in the garden.

Our herbs may be annuals, perennials, biennials, bulbs, shrubs, trees, vines, or aquatics. We value their flowers and leaves, their bark and berries, their tastes and scents. Some are relatively new to cultivation, while others enjoy herbal pedigrees dating back to the beginnings of civilization. Their stories fascinate us. This historical resonance is part of the charm of many of the plants we grow. More than that, we've come to associate certain plants with our families and friends, thereby creating our own herbal traditions. We plant at certain times, harvest at certain times, and applaud the first batch of gazpacho. There's always something to celebrate in the garden.

Herbs have become an integral part of our world, or at least the world we've created in our garden. Although we do more sweating than sitting, we occasionally find the time to stop and appreciate our achievement. We read the paper, shell peas, or listen to music on the patio. We entertain friends. Woodpeckers, hummingbirds, and butterflies entertain us. Sometimes we simply watch the sun come up over the garden or set behind it.

Why do we garden? Because it's what we do. Now we'd like to share what we've learned about growing herbs and the art of intermingling them with other plants in the garden.

Chapter 1

FOLIAGE FIRST

IN ANY LANDSCAPE, the gardener may be tempted to make plant choices based on flower color. Sometimes, even when the flower combinations seem perfect, the effect is still unsatisfying, and the gardener wonders why. More often than not, the problem is one of architecture, not color. One of the simplest ways to create a boring garden is to put in plants whose leaves all look alike. Foliage makes up the bulk of the landscape. Here is where the varied shapes and textures of herbs—which as a rule are grown more for their leaves than their blossoms—can make strong contributions in every season.

If you anchor a bed with a variety of good, bold foliage plants, it looks as though something is going on there. A garden that relies solely on flowers is in big trouble during those dreaded periods when little is in bloom. A display of good foliage helps a garden get through the dull times more gracefully.

Foliage color is as important as foliage texture. Contrasting and complementing plants with blue, bronze, burgundy, and silver leaves can create effects that rival the best schemes based on flower color. The blue sheen of 'African Blue' basil, the burgundy shades of perilla or red orach, the stunning silver of artemisias and lamiums, and the invigorating mint green of golden hops can each add depth, drama, and highlights to a garden. All together they may look like the dog's dinner, so it's worth considering them separately before attempting combinations.

GOLD, CHARTREUSE, AND MINT GREEN

The first leaves of spring seem the most precious, especially to gardeners who have just been through a bleak, nearly lifeless winter. Even in the South and along the West Coast, where seasonal changes are less pronounced, emerging shoots of lettuce signal a period of renewal and growth. The lovely gold and chartreuse of many young leaves doesn't last long, and most gardens green up quickly. Herbs that can remind us of spring later in the season or break up the monotony of summer green are invaluable in any setting. They enhance the colors of neighboring plants and contribute to a livelier garden picture.

Some "gold" plants aren't truly gold but rather a yellow-green that nevertheless stands out among other garden greens. Some could be described as spring green, lime, or apple green. A few gold-leaved herbs, such as golden comfrey (*Symphytum grandiflorum* 'Gold in Spring' or 'Belsay Gold') or golden valerian (*Valeriana phu* 'Aurea'), make such a strong

The point is dramatic: Yucca filamentosa *'Golden Sword' paired with the plush leaves of* Stachys byzantina *'Helene von Stein', often sold under the unfortunate name 'Big Ears'.*

For the repressed modern artist in us all: a composition of non-blooming
lamb's ears (Stachys byzantina *'Silver Carpet'*)*, Geranium cinereum, thyme,*
and golden hops vine employed as a ground cover.

statement that it's difficult to ignore them (though their coloration often reverts to green later in the growing season).

Golden feverfew (*Tanacetum parthenium* 'Aureum') grabs the spotlight anywhere in the garden. We use it lavishly—perhaps to excess—because of its ease of cultivation and, of course, propagation. We first planted it in the shade garden, where its ruffly lime foliage makes a textural contrast with the bold gold-edged *Hosta* 'Frances Williams' and the linear fountains of variegated lilyturf (*Liriope spicata* 'Silvery Sunproof'), which we grow in shade despite its name to keep the yellow-streaked blades from scorching. It was not long before we transplanted feverfew seedlings to the blue and yellow border, where their lime foliage contributes as much as the blue flowers of veronicas and nepetas and yellow blooms of lilies and heleniums that it was meant to complement.

The next logical place for a good jolt of golden feverfew was among the vegetables. Whether or not feverfew's bitter taste actually repels insects, the golden leaves look great with ripening plum tomatoes, variegated nasturtiums, and lemongrass. We are in danger of getting carried away by such a good thing, and it won't be long before golden feverfew pops up, either by plan or by accident, among our pots or on the compost heap.

Our enthusiasm for golden hops vine (*Humulus lupulus* 'Aureus') is nearly as rampant. Our first plant was an experiment—a successful one, as it turned out—to integrate vines into the perennial border. The vine twines through and over a grouping of blue anchusas, irises, caryopterises, nigellas, and catmints; magenta cranesbills, lilies, silenes, and coneflowers; and pale yellow *Dianthus knappii*, giant yellow scabiouses (*Cephalaria alpina*), and straw foxgloves (*Digitalis lutea*). The golden hops doesn't calm the mixture, but does provide a note

of continuity as it scrambles through the plants (sometimes too aggressively), setting off the glowing flowers as it goes. We could not resist turning hops loose on the blue and yellow border and then the shade garden, following the path of the golden feverfew seedlings in reverse. Now we're considering unleashing it on some neighbor's cars in the alley. Golden hops have an iron constitution, flourishing in sun or shade, but the leaves can burn in the hot sun, especially when sufficient moisture isn't available.

Golden lemon balm (*Melissa officinalis* 'Aurea') offers the same light, lemony scent of its plain green counterpart but grows somewhat less aggressively. We banned green lemon balm from our garden after it began to take hostages, but the golden form has earned a spot hemmed in by paving stones where we can keep it under surveillance.

Golden thymes are fairly drought tolerant, but we try not to push it. Drying winter winds periodically damage or kill some of our thyme plants, but replacements are easy to propagate. As lime green carpets at the front of perennial beds, they enhance the blossoms of cranesbills, penstemons, sunroses, and irises, especially the yellow-striped foliage of *Iris pallida* 'Aurea Variegata'. Low-growing, spreading clumps of golden oregano (*Origanum vulgare* 'Aureum') serve a similar purpose, but because the leaves are larger, the effect is quite different. The blazing sun can blowtorch its foliage, so we water often or plant it in partial shade. The golden comfreys *S. g.* 'Gold in Spring' and *S.* 'Belsay Gold' also belong in the shade, with brilliant yellow-green foliage complementing daffodils, grape hyacinths, and wood hyacinths.

Golden Irish moss (*Sagina subulata* 'Aurea') matches the intense coloration of the golden comfreys but with tiny leaves of a contrasting texture. Although we use the moss primarily between paving stones in

> The varied shapes and textures of herbs—which as a rule are grown more for their leaves than their blossoms—can make strong contributions in every season.

moist areas, it's also ideal to help carpet the ground among shade-loving herbs, flowers, and shrubs. Equally useful for brightening shady areas are golden moneywort (*Lysimachia nummularia* 'Aurea') and golden cultivars of *Lamium maculatum*. The former is persistent and rambunctious but relatively

harmless, while the latter is a reluctant grower for us, preferring a wetter climate. Another golden refugee from a moist climate is the sweet potato

The striped seedpods of love-in-a-mist contrast effectively with the foliage of Ballota *'All Hallow's Green'.*

Ipomoea batatas 'Sulfur'. Sweet potatoes consort so beautifully with herbs that we include them in our plantings. The leaves of 'Sulfur' are less divided than those of the popular maroon 'Blackie' and make a startling contrast with variegated and silver herbs. The bold yellow-green holds throughout the summer and echoes that of golden barberry or golden spirea in the mixed border. We let the sweet potato scramble through the beds.

Lady's mantle (*Alchemilla mollis*), with those beautifully scalloped, dew-catching leaves, is a superior foliage plant throughout the year, but its sprays of airy chartreuse blossoms make it indispensable for bringing out the best in other plants. Every party—whether in the garden or not— needs a guest like lady's mantle, in whose company the catnips glow a little brighter, the sweet Williams look more dapper, the bellflowers shine more radiantly. This sociable behavior almost excuses the promiscuous self-seeding of lady's mantle, a habit that is sharply curbed in dry climates like ours in Denver.

Another herb with outstanding yellow flowers has been overshadowed by lady's mantle in flower gardens, even though it blooms for a longer period and makes a bigger show. Lady's bedstraw (*Galium verum*) used to be an important strewing herb. These days, few of us stuff our mattresses or cover our kitchen floors with aromatic herbs (although we're considering it to hide the tomato sauce stains). But then again, few of us try our hand at alchemy to turn the dewdrops of lady's mantle into precious metal. This transformation didn't work four hundred years ago, but lady's mantle still kept her place in the herb garden; lady's bedstraw lost hers. It hardly seems fair. Lady's bedstraw forms an impressive, nonspreading clump that produces a froth of yellow flowers with a lime cast on stems up to 3 feet high in early to midsummer. Easy to grow in sun in most any soil, this long-lived perennial stays attractive as the flowers fade from yellow to chartreuse to pale green. Although a rain shower can make the whole plant flop like a wet tent, a peony hoop or supporting structure of wire or brush keeps this from happening. We use lady's bedstraw to complement wood betony, blue avena grass, garden sage, and lavender. There must be a hundred other ways to exploit the extraordinary color.

The bracts of alexanders (*Smyrnium perfoliatum*) are such an intense lemon-lime that they threaten to upstage even such vivid spring flowers as tulips or honesty. Growing from 2 to 4 feet tall, this wispy biennial has the uncanny knack of seeding itself in all the right places. Sometimes called black

*A trellis of golden hops vine frames a view of drifts of lavender,
bistort, lily of the valley, sweet cicely, and artemisia.*

lovage because of its black seeds, it closely resembles *Bupleurum* 'Green Gold', another self-sowing biennial member of the carrot family that blooms in early summer. Its showy bracts of acidic greenish yellow make an extraordinary complement to the Spode blue of peach-leaf bellflower (*Campanula persicifolia*).

Other chartreuse accents come from the understated beauty of dill, mustard, and arugula flowers. We let all three seed patches in the vegetable plot and allow dill to roam a bit further, wherever its finely cut leaves and attractive umbels complement their companions without overshadowing them. Dill and other carrot-family members are important food sources for the larvae of swallowtail butterflies, another reason we like to have plenty around.

Mint-green leaves don't have the pizzazz that bolder chartreuse ones do, but their good looks invite pleasing, softer combinations. *Stachys byzantina* 'Primrose Heron' is the color of a lemon-lime sherbet or perhaps pistachio pudding and adds a note that is cool and refreshing in front of cranesbills, mallows, and scabious. Gardeners have just begun to discover how to use this pastel hue. Seemingly as hardy as other varieties of lamb's ears, 'Primrose Heron' appears to be the least invasive of the lot, no doubt a blessing for most of us. It seldom flowers.

The color of *Helichrysum petiolare* 'Limelight' is slightly more intense than that of 'Primrose Heron'. Sometimes called licorice plant, this vigorous, tender sprawler (grown as an annual in all but frost-free climates) has small, felted, oval leaves. It's seen more often in containers than in the border but looks great in either. 'Splash' combines the best of 'Limelight' and the gray-leaved species, and in itself is highly ornamental.

The pistachio-pudding color also occurs in the foliage of tangerine southernwood

> Every party—whether in the garden or not—needs a guest like lady's mantle, in whose company the catnips glow a little brighter, the sweet Williams look more dapper, the bellflowers shine more radiantly.

(*Artemisia abrotanum* var. *limoneum*), dittany of Crete, mountain mints such as *Pycnanthemum virginianum* (a favorite of herbal wreath makers for the extraordinary peppermint aroma), and certain ballotas and marrubiums (horehounds). The last two, which are lovely plants, grow best in relatively dry climates where they can spill over rocks or onto paths. *Ballota pseudodictamnus* makes a spreading mound of trailing stems with thick, rounded leaves of silvery green and tiny lavender flowers. *B.* 'All Hallow's Green', found in an Irish garden by the eminent plantswoman Valerie Finnis, boasts rounded, felty leaves of mint green on mounded plants about a foot high. Silver-edged horehound (*Marrubium rotundifolium*), a Turkish native, has thick, felty green leaves with bright white edges and white woolly undersides. The foliage is about 10 inches high with taller spikes of creamy white flowers arranged in tiers like those of true horehound (*M. vulgare*). The puckered gray-green leaves of horehound contrast nicely with white bellflowers or Greek yarrow (*Achillea ageratifolia*). We used to let the flower spikes dry on the plant until we discovered all the seedlings that resulted.

The pale olive leaves of sweet Annie (*Artemisia annua*) are as fine and lacy as they come, with an irresistible fruity fragrance that makes them a favorite for potpourri and wreath weaving. To retain the best color, veteran wreath makers advise cutting and drying the foliage before the flowers open. The tall, gawky stalks add height and fine texture at the back of a planting. A similar effect comes from dog fennel (*Eupatorium capillifolium*), a southeastern native that's had a tough time getting admitted to proper gardens. North Carolina plantswomen Edith Eddleman and Kim Hawks have taken a liking to it. Its lanky, arching branches with thin, pale sage green

We believe in an overstuffed garden, exemplified by our planting of lady's mantle, catmint, yellow foxglove, peach-leaf bellflower, and Stachys grandiflora.

leaves like Spanish moss grow 6 to 10 feet tall by late summer and autumn, when its shaggy-dog presence complements late rudbeckias, cannas, and ornamental grasses. Perhaps other gardeners will follow suit.

THE BEAUTY OF BRONZE

Dark leaves intrigue us. A rare sight barely a decade ago, plants with bronze foliage now play an increasingly important role in garden design. Shades vary from red and purple to burgundy, brown, and nearly black. As both backdrops and accents, dark-leaved herbs offer gardeners the opportunity to stretch their creativity in designing combinations. A single dark-toned plant interrupts the complacent eye as it scans a garden, just as a variegated, silver, or chartreuse plant does. Whereas the latter create highlights, dark plants create shadows. Both effects have a place.

Our enthusiasm for bronze-leaved plants started almost by accident with the acquisition of pincushion flower (*Knautia macedonica*), a perennial related to scabious with burgundy flowers and ordinary green foliage. As we looked for a way to make the most of the flowers' deep hue, we found it too intense to pair with pastels (blood-red roses often pose the same problem). Then we thought that perhaps bronze fennel might be an effective foil to the pincushion flowers, and a floodgate of ideas opened. A young smokebush (*Cotinus coggygria* 'Royal Purple') joined the fray, as did the violet flowers of *Salvia forskaohlei*, *Geranium platypetalum*, meadow rue, red dianthus, and deep pink Jupiter's beard. *Anthriscus sylvestris* 'Ravenswing' fit in near the front, but its deep bronze, feathery leaves almost disappeared against bare earth, so *Sedum* × 'Vera Jameson', whose fleshy gray leaves have a purple cast, got stuffed in as well.

We've added wine red *Clematis* 'Niobe', maroon bearded iris, purple sage, and 'Blackie' sweet potato. The result is a splendid portion of the border—*and* a splendid setting for the pincushion flowers.

The success of this border has led us to include bronze accents in other areas. If purple sage (*Salvia officinalis* 'Purpureus') posted a better survival rate in our winters, we'd probably use it in dozens of spots. We envy our friends in mild climates who use great mounds of its softly textured smoky-toned leaves to anchor masses of Japanese anemones, Russian sage, joe-pye weed, and other statuesque perennials. In our gardens, we settle for small accent clumps of purple sage, replacing them in the spring if necessary, and let bronze fennel seed itself wherever its somber-toned foliage will enhance adjacent flowers. One caveat: the pale sulfur blooms atop the burgundy haze of leaves can sometimes skew an intended color scheme.

Few plants catch the attention of our visitors as quickly as red orach (*Atriplex hortensis* 'Rubra'). It's splendid but no floral beauty. We keep digging up seedlings and sending them out to colonize other people's gardens. When red orach sprouts (as it does in great numbers), the leaves are already deep beet red, fabulous as a carpet beneath scarlet tulips. It shoots up quickly to about 5 feet tall, producing insignificant blossoms that mature into flat, round seeds as dark as the foliage. Why we—and everybody else—like this old-fashioned European salad and tonic herb as much as we do is a mystery. We spend far too much time each spring thinning the seedlings, roguing out greenish plants that dilute the deep color of our colony, and questioning our sanity. Golden orach (*A. h.* 'Aureus') grows on the other side of the garden (its foliage color is most attractive in early summer when the yellow foxgloves bloom), but we hope the day never comes when these strains mate. We envision a horrid orange muddle like the skin of a *Star Trek* alien.

Early summer marks the zenith of red loosestrife (*Lysimachia ciliata* 'Rubra').

Borne on 2-foot stems, the deep maroon leaves and clusters of tiny yellow flowers add richness when planted behind the flowers of coral bells, monarda, and Jupiter's beard. The maroon is apparent as soon as shoots emerge in spring, making this loosestrife an ideal companion for spring bulbs, especially purple-mottled *Tulipa greigii* cultivars such as pink-flowered 'Sweet Lady' and scarlet 'Red Riding Hood'. Like almost every other bronze plant we like, it spreads too well, but since it's relatively shallow-rooted, most of its companions compete favorably. We don't lose any sleep over its invasiveness.

The dark forms of the annual *Perilla frutescens* look a bit like their coleus cousins, but the deep maroon leaves have a metallic glint. This Southeast Asian native has no trouble reseeding after a cold winter. It's fortunate that this herb looks handsome with so many plants because it's firmly established in several parts of our garden. It's also lucky that we have a strain whose leaves hold their deep maroon throughout the season: some lose their good color and turn green halfway through the summer. We're also growing a super form with extremely dark leaves that we collected in a Massachusetts garden. It reaches 3 feet in Denver, but nearly 6 in the humid East. It blooms very late, though, and because the seeds don't always ripen before our first frost, we usually pull a pot inside to mature. It's worth the trouble for this superior strain, which we've dubbed "Perilla deVil". The taste of shiso, as it's called in Japanese cuisine, doesn't appeal to everyone, but we like it.

The classic Italian basil, *Ocimum basilicum*, is available in several dark cultivars, including 'Red Rubin' and 'Purple Ruffles'. They are as versatile as perilla in the landscape but without the self-sown seedlings. Their foliage complements eggplant, tricolor sage, and lemon mint (*Monarda citriodora*) and contrasts strikingly with silver-leaved plants such as pinks, society garlic, and dusty miller.

A combination of 'Red Rubin' basil, dusty miller, and the white form of Salvia farinacea *helps dismiss the notion that annual designs lack sophistication.*

Our quest for exciting bronze plants continues. Bronze-leaf elder (*Sambucus nigra* 'Guincho Purple') and purple-leaf sand cherry (*Prunus × cistena*) make impressive backdrops. Red-leaf rose (*Rosa glauca*) offers smoky gray leaves with burgundy undersides. On a smaller scale, red barberry bushes are easily integrated into a mixed border.

Several grasses with bronze foliage—*Pennisetum setaceum* 'Rubrum' and 'Burgundy Giant' and Japanese blood grass (*Imperata cylindrica* 'Red Baron')—make effective linear accents for many herbs. Bauer's dracaena (*Cordyline baueri*) adds a spiky structure with leaves nearly the color of a chocolate bar. Grown as perennials on the West Coast and elsewhere as annuals, the several bronze cultivars of New Zealand flax (*Phormium tenax*) spell drama in a big way, presiding high above lavenders, santolina, and gazanias.

Opportunities to use bronze leaves abound throughout the garden. For quick excitement, two annuals bear consideration. Prince's-feather (*Amaranthus hypochondriacus*) grows up to 4 feet tall with beet red leaves and irregular pyramidal flower heads of royal burgundy, as though a sumac has been grafted atop a stem of red orach. The dark-leaved form of castor bean (*Ricinus communis*) might easily be dubbed the queen of bronze foliage. (Parents of young children may want to avoid this plant because its beans are poisonous.) It grows so fast that it could be considered an annual tree. With heat and moisture, castor bean adds panache to borders—or use the plants to hide your neighbor's Winnebago.

THE SUBJECT OF SILVER

Herb gardens have long served as repositories for plants with silver leaves. In the past few decades, designers discovering the delightful ornamental attributes of silver have liberated these plants from the herb garden. Santolina, thyme, and southernwood have become so popular as landscape plants that some people have no inkling of their long herbal histories. Other silver-leaved plants such as lamb's ears and partridge feather have found homes in herb gardens with few questions asked, gaining herb status from the explosion of interest in drying plants for wreaths, potpourris, sachets, and arrangements—for which they are ideal.

We find gray-leaved plants immensely attractive. Most are covered with pale hairs—a product of evolution that enables them to cope with hot, dry climates. They shield the leaves from the sun, as hair protects the scalp, and trap moisture. Leaf hairs reflect sunlight, giving plants the appearance of silver. Many gray leaves are small or narrow or, like those of many artemisias, finely dissected, exposing the least surface to burn in the sun or desiccate in the wind. In addition, many of these

In the courtyard at Chanticleer in Pennsylvania, water drips from a venerable cauldron surrounded by Artemisia *'Powis Castle', dahlias,* Verbena patagonica, *peppers, and 'Blackie' sweet potato.*

plants contain bitter oils that discourage chewing or sucking insects and animals.

As garden plants, the silvers attract few pests (who wants a nasty-tasting mouthful of hair?) and often demonstrate superior drought tolerance. Their only real enemy is humid, wet weather, which can rot the roots

A study in silver at the Portland garden of Sean Hogan and Parker Sanderson includes curry plant, pearly everlasting, felt-white Senecio vera-vera, *and* Rosa sericea *var.* pteracantha, *noted for its ow!-inspiring thorns.*

or disfigure the foliage. Muggy summers may preclude successfully growing many of these plants in much of eastern North America.

Artemisias rank as one of the biggest, most adaptable groups of silver herbs. The hybrid wormwoods *Artemisia* 'Huntington' and 'Powis Castle' perform reliably in the Midwest, on the East Coast, and even in the South, forming fine-textured silver pillows several feet high and more than a yard across. Most authorities rate these superior wormwoods as hardy only to Zone 6 or 7, but we've found that they're reliably hardy several zones colder if grown in lean, well-drained soil. True wormwood (*A. absinthium*) makes a similar silver cloud and is hardy to Zone 4. Like most other species of *Artemisia*, it has a bitter taste and is a powerful deterrent to both insects and animals. The cultivar 'Lambrook Silver' is more compact than the species and has finely cut silver leaves. 'Huntington', 'Powis Castle', and 'Lambrook Silver' grow like shrubs. We cut them back almost to the ground each spring to encourage thick, bushy growth and to keep them in bounds.

Prairie sage (*A. ludoviciana*) is a runner. The cultivars 'Silver King' and 'Silver Queen' behave like medieval monarchs, invading new territories with a vengeance. To thwart their aggression, we confine them to a bottomless bucket set in the garden soil just up to its rim, where their royal charms—straight stems up to 4 feet tall clad in downy gray leaves and topped by pyramids of tiny flowers—can best be appreciated. 'Valerie Finnis' also runs rampant when given the opportunity but may be somewhat inhibited by stiff competition from other tough perennials, merely threading through them with its attractive 3-foot stalks of broad, almost white leaves. A bucket solves any problem before it starts.

Roman wormwood (*A. pontica*) grows only 15 inches tall (less in the compact 'Nana'), but its spread can be measured in miles rather than inches. It makes a good ground cover in tough areas, but gardeners who tend small plots should get out the bucket. Our friends Sean Hogan and Parker Sanderson in Portland, Oregon, use ferny, greenish gray Roman wormwood to great effect beneath towering shrub roses and ornamental grasses, where the herb fills in and spars with mints and lamb's ears for dominance.

Few gardeners can complain about the habits of stay-put *A. schmidtiana* 'Silver Mound', except that its pretty dome often collapses at the height of the season. Keep it

Cyclamens dance above the irregularly-striped leaves of Stachys
byzantina *'Phantom'. The name is unintentionally appropriate as the variegation
sometimes disappears when plain gray leaves reassert themselves.*

in poor soil with no additional organic matter and no other moisture than what falls from the sky, and it will stay a compact silver mound instead of a silver mess. Most artemisias need very little moisture or fertilizer, and too much of either will kill them outright or lead

Double-flowered chamomile, above, accents silver-edged horehound and dunesilver. Billowing silver clouds of Artemisia *'Powis Castle', right, set off* Sedum spectabilis *'Autumn Joy' and dianthus.*

to an early death. Fringed sage (*A. frigida*) thrives on neglect and forms short clumps of filigreed branches about a foot tall. California sagebrush (*A. californica*) offers lacy, pewter gray leaves on shrubby plants up to 5 feet tall. The compact, garden-worthy selections 'Canyon Grey' and 'Montara' stay under 2 feet tall. Another excellent choice for West Coast gardens is native sandhill sage (*A. pycnocephala*), a handsome mound former. The compact

selection 'David's Choice', less than a foot tall with feathery, dark gray foliage, often survives as far north as Zone 5. Lucky us.

Dunesilver, or beach wormwood (*A. stelleriana*) sprawls along the ground with pinnate, nearly white leaves. The cultivar 'Silver Brocade' stays particularly short and compact. An especially good companion is *Sedum spurium* 'Red Carpet', whose fleshy, beet red leaves make a strong contrast with the felty white ones of 'Silver Brocade'.

We've also gone crazy for *A. armeniaca*, a small shrub less than a foot tall with thin, curled leaves that look like frosted reindeer moss. We feature it near the edges of borders where autumn crocus and Johnny-jump-ups can pop up beneath its oddly intriguing foliage.

If we had to single out one group of plants for their nonstop contribution to the garden, it would be the simple pinks. Attractive, nearly pest-free foliage is only one of their many attributes. The common name for many species of *Dianthus* may come not from the color (although many pinks *are* pink) but from the fringed petals that appear to have been pinked by shears. Pinks can play an important role in almost any garden—in front of sunny borders, edging paths, and in rock and wall gardens. The charming flowers of many forms are both fragrant and edible and impart their spiciness to beverages, which is why one of their folk names is sops-in-wine. Sun, well-drained soil, and a lean diet suit most species.

Pinks look great with nearly every other garden plant and their rounded mounds of gray give a good account in every season. The only work involved in caring for them is to shear off the blossoms after the main flush of bloom in early summer. We have thought of investing in electric clippers just for this purpose because we grow so many pinks and they keep adding to their

At the heady altitude of over 7,800 feet in Aspen, Colorado, this garden of feverfew, delphinium, Maltese cross, Indian blanket, sweet Williams, lavender, and lamb's ears takes advantage of an enviable curtain of blue mountains.

numbers by self-sowing. Selected forms are easily increased by rooting cuttings. Southern gardeners have rarely had much success with pinks because the plants resent hot, humid conditions, but 'Bath's Pink', a pretty selection from Georgia with pale pink single flowers and blue-green leaves, has changed that. The other gray-leaved selections, however, still perform best above the Mason-Dixon Line.

Cottage pinks are descended mainly from the European species *D. plumarius*, a mound-former with narrow gray leaves and pink flowers. They may have single, semidouble, or double blossoms in white, pink, or reddish pink, often with an eye of a contrasting color. Because *Dianthus* species cross freely, it is nearly impossible to keep up with the hybrids, but those of note include double white 'Mrs. Sinkins' and 'Agatha', which is deep pink with a crimson eye.

The Allwood hybrids (*D. × allwoodii*) were created by crossing cottage pinks with carnations (*D. caryophyllus*). With blue-gray leaves and scented flowers that often resemble small carnations, these plants grow a foot tall or slightly higher. 'Daphne' has single, pale pink flowers with a darker pink center. 'Essex Witch' bears semidouble, finely fringed pink flowers, while those of 'Helen' are salmon pink. 'Ian' produces double red blossoms edged with crimson, and 'Timothy' is pink speckled with red.

Cheddar pinks (*D. gratianopolitanus*) form rounded mounds of blue-gray linear leaves up to a foot tall. The strongly scented pink blossoms appear in early summer. A diminutive selection called 'Tiny Rubies' has double bright pink blossoms and gray-green foliage.

Few plants deliver as much bloom, fragrance, and satisfaction as blue catmint (*Nepeta × faassenii*). Its 15-inch-high mound of rounded gray-green leaves puts out a prolific first flush of sterile lavender-blue blooms in early summer and again later if deadheaded promptly.

Many gardeners, especially in western states, have taken a keen interest in unusual species of catmint from western Asia. Our friend Marcia Tatroe has championed them because they tolerate the clay soil, high alkalinity, and low rainfall of our area. She tries every species for which she can obtain seed (such as through the annual seed exchange of the North American Rock Garden Society, which in 1997 listed more than 6,000 species of plants). Several years ago, she planted out a dozen seedlings of new catmint species for trial in a freshly dug bed. Later that day, her industrious husband, Randy, believing that the bed needed more work and unaware that Marcia had just set out her tiny rarities, rototilled the whole kit and caboodle under. Her trials with the catmints were delayed; however, plants of three species were not in the bed that got plowed and—oddly enough—they are three that we had also raised from seed.

After several seasons in both gardens, we can recommend them all. *N. phylloclamys* has brilliant, downy white leaves on ground-hugging stems and small lavender-blue flowers. It reseeds itself well, which is a good thing since a soggy, cold winter sometimes kills mature plants. *N. sibthorpii* forms a low mound of gray-green leaves like miniature lamb's ears and sends up short spikes, to a foot tall, with small pink blossoms. It self-seeds nominally. *N. dirphya* is vase-shaped in full bloom with small white blossoms on stems held above rounded gray-green leaves. Not the showiest of the catmints, it has a yummy fragrance that appears to hold no interest for neighborhood tabbies.

*I*f we had to single out one group of plants for their nonstop contribution to the garden, it would be the simple pinks.

The excellent sagelike foliage and foot-tall, bright blue spikes of silver speedwell (*Veronica incana*) have been a favorite of ours for years. Not quite as drought tolerant as its leaves might suggest, silver speedwell forced us to experiment to find the balance between frying it and rotting it. We've settled on a lean, well-drained soil in full sun that receives supplemental moisture only during the hottest, driest spells. Gray speedwell (*V. cinerea*) exhibits greater drought tolerance and appears unfazed by blazing heat. At just 6 inches high with a spread of up to 2 feet, gray speedwell imitates the needlelike leaves of pinks but surprises us with small spikes of smoky blue flowers in early summer. It's great for rock gardens and path or border edging.

Curry plants (*Helichrysum italicum* and *H. splendidum*) are valued for their intense aroma and spicy taste in chicken, cheese, or egg dishes, as well as for the narrow, ornamental, bright gray leaves and cream-colored flower heads. Although curry plant smells like traditional Indian curry seasoning, it's not the same. Curry powder is a blend containing—but not limited to—ginger, coriander, cardamom, cayenne pepper, and turmeric. How odd that one plant could embody the collective scent of at least five others!

Licorice plant (*H. petiolare*, not related to the true source of licorice, *Glycyrrhiza glabra*) has become a favorite sprawler for beds, pots, and hanging baskets. Its small, rounded gray leaves with their felty texture can't be beat for bringing out the best in other plants. Even potted geraniums and marguerite daisies become suddenly chic when paired with licorice plant.

While small leaves and fine texture are prime characteristics of gray-leaved plants, a few feature much broader foliage. These plants make especially appealing focal points in the garden. Silver clary (*Salvia argentea*) forms a rosette of leaves as much as a foot long and half again as wide. The covering of long white hairs looks as though it would be easy to comb and style; this salvia seems more Muppet than plant. A 2-foot candelabra inflorescence of white flowers rises from the rosette in its second season, after which it often dies unless grown on the dry side.

Much tougher and longer lived are two salvias that look alike. *S. frigida* is smaller but its leaves stay evergreen (or evergray) even in our cold winters, whereas *S. argentea* loses most of its foliage. This miniature version, with white flowers on a foot-tall spike in June, is perfect for the rock garden or a position near the front of a water-wise border. So is *S. candidissima* from Turkey, which is similar in all respects to *S. frigida* except that its leaves are quite hairy and it blooms a month earlier.

S. clevelandii is a shrubby plant growing 4 to 5 feet tall with sky blue flowers set against gray leaves scented like hand lotion. It grows best on the West Coast. The true species is rarely seen in cultivation; a hybrid has supplanted it in commerce and is superior in size, scent, and silveriness. A choice shrubby salvia that performs without flaw on the West Coast and in much of the South is Mexican bush sage (*S. leucantha*), which has deep olive green leaves with downy, bright white undersides. It grows to 2 or 3

feet tall and is crowned with downy purple-and-white flowers from summer late into autumn.

Cardoon (*Cynara cardunculus*) and artichoke (*C. scolymus*) also form attractive rosettes. Their bold gray-green, thistly foliage is an excellent antidote to a grouping containing only plants with small leaves. The lavender flowers and seed heads are a bonus. Cardoon and artichoke make compelling specimens in vegetable and herb gardens as well as perennial borders. They revel in warm weather but need regular moisture to thrive. A recent artichoke, 'Imperial Star', matures in 90 to 100 days to allow short-season northern gardeners to harvest their own tasty crop.

Sea kale (*Crambe maritima*) also provides a bold accent. Bearing tints of aqua, the blue-gray leaves give off an iridescent sheen in certain light conditions. Sea kale makes a season-long contribution unless the grasshoppers get at the cabbagelike foliage. The creamy white flowers, borne like tufts of broccoli on stiff stems, rise above the foliage in late spring. As one might imagine, sea kale grows best in sandy, well-drained soil.

Clumps of grasses with bluish leaves complement silver herbs and contribute to the structure of a planting. European dune grass, also called blue lyme grass (*Elymus glaucus*), has broad blades of an excellent steely blue that may help a gardener forgive its aggressive spreading (it makes a good inmate in a bucket). By contrast, the very narrow leaves of blue fescue (*Festuca glauca*) form an 8-inch-tall clump that never gets out of bounds. The very blue 'Elijah Blue' and the dwarf green 'Sea Urchin' offer nice variation. Blue avena grass (*Helictotrichon sempervirens*) combines beautifully with many herbs and ornamental flowers, forming a noninvasive clump about 2 feet tall, gracefully accented by its blond seed heads in midsummer.

> **Cardoon and artichoke make compelling specimens in vegetable and herb gardens as well as perennial borders.**

Gardeners who pay attention to foliage effects create combinations far different from those that can be achieved with flowers. The leaves of milk thistle reveal their metallic silver pattern startlingly against bronze Heuchera *'Palace Purple'.*

Several annual and biennial plants also contribute attractive gray leaves to the garden scene. Dusty millers are an obvious choice, particularly selections such as the deeply lobed *Senecio cineraria* 'Silverdust' and broad-leaf 'Cirrus'. 'Silver Cloud' is a cultivar of *Tanacetum ptarmiciflorum*. We find it more difficult to germinate, and it's a finicky transplanter, but the extremely finely cut, feathery foliage makes it worth the effort.

The relatively broad, smooth gray-green leaves of opium poppy (*Papaver somniferum*) enhance its pretty, delicate flowers, although it's undeniably the flowers that account for its popularity. Sunflower (*Helianthus annuus*) lovers welcome the silver-leaved cultivars such as 'Silverleaf' wherever they need a tall, robust backdrop. The magenta, white, or blush pink flowers of rose campion (*Lychnis coronaria*) would be far less notable without the woolly silver leaves. The woolliest of all plants in our garden is silver mullein (*Verbascum bombycifer-*

um 'Arctic Summer'). Its thick, basal rosettes appear to have been cut from a warm blanket. In its second year, the flowering spikes growing 5 feet tall or more are clad in white cotton, accenting the lemon yellow flowers.

THE VALUE OF VARIEGATION

Variegated leaves have long fascinated gardeners. They come in many patterns, from stripes and edgings to spots and splashes. Most plants normally have solid-colored leaves, with a variegated form only occasionally popping up either from natural mutation or from viral infection. Keen gardeners spot the variegated seedling or offshoot, then carefully propagate the sport to share it with others. Because less of a variegated leaf is devoted to photosynthesis (white areas contain no chlorophyll), most variegated plants are less vigorous than their plain green counterparts and may need

ROB'S LEAF AFFAIR

I don't suppose anyone starts gardening because they love foliage. I fell for flowers at an early age and never recovered; few things thrill me as much as the spring appearance of Corvette-red tulips or the scent of a plump, old-fashioned rose. Along the way, however, I've come to appreciate that leaves are the solar collectors that make the flowers possible. Now I understand how much richer and more diverse the garden is when I pay attention to the leaves. Big, small, fuzzy, shiny, puckered, and pleated, leaves provide an almost infinite opportunity for artful combinations.

This fascination with leaves has led me quite naturally to fancy-leaf and scented geraniums. I'm not yet the expert that my friend Helen Dillon is; she had collected forty varieties of fancy-leaf and scented geraniums by the time she was fourteen. This Irishwoman grew up to become one of the world's most esteemed plantswomen, admired for her impeccably artistic garden.

I've yet to reach forty in my own *Pelargonium* collection, but I'm working on it. Many of the old-time fancy-leaf and scented geraniums have fallen victim to horticultural fashion, and very few were available until fairly recently. Now there's an incredible resurgence of interest in their leafy charms.

One of my favorites is 'Chocolate Mint', a scented variety with fuzzy green leaves marked with a central brown patch. I'm also partial to the old fancy-leaf 'Skies of Italy' with bands of green, white, and brownish red, apparently named for the stripes on the Italian flag. This was the first fancy-leaf type I bought, and I keep it going by taking cuttings each fall. I do the same with favorite scented types that I experiment with as they appear in mail-order catalogs. Not every variety impresses me enough to winter over. Competition is fierce on the windowsills and under fluorescent lights. Every so often, I'm forced to purge the collection of the poorest performers and the worst whitefly magnets. Sometimes I even throw out a rare but homely variety, despite the fact that it took years to track down and cost too much.

It's so easy to become a crazed collector. Many people feel the compulsive urge to amass stuff, whether plants, dolls, or saltshakers. Thankfully, I don't have room for the latter two, because the house is full of geraniums.

extra coddling. This can seem unlikely to a gardener whose territory has been invaded by gardener's garters (*Phalaris arundinacea* 'Picta') or variegated bishop's weed (*Aegopodium podagraria* 'Variegatum'). Any offshoot with all-white leaves can't survive if detached from the mother plant because it's unable to manufacture food.

Our garden boasts many plants with variegated leaves, but not all of our gardening friends understand our enthusiasm. "Here's another sick plant for you," crowed our friend Tom as he arrived with a pelargonium he'd found that had produced a stem with cream marbling its otherwise green foliage. Gardeners of the Victorian era were among the first to become intrigued by variegated leaves, and pelargoniums supplied them with plenty of examples. Dozens—even hundreds—of fancy-leaf and scented geraniums were grown during their heyday. Some had edges of white or green, while others displayed bands of cream and chartreuse that alternated with green, red, or brown. Flowers were of secondary importance; one variety was reputed not to bloom at all.

These plants were employed in elaborate bedding schemes, lined along walks, or displayed in urns. Unfortunately, only a fraction of these old sports survived fashion changes during the first half of this century. A resurgence of interest in variegation, especially in scented geraniums, has rescued some heirloom varieties from the brink of extinction, while new ones have popped up or been bred.

The interest in variegated herbs grows. Some are herbaceous, while others are shrubs or vines. Perhaps they surprise and delight us because variegation takes an ordinary green leaf (or occasionally a gray, gold, or bronze one) and outlines it in a crisp edge or paints it with an intricate pattern or runs a dramatic stripe across it. We're suddenly compelled to examine a leaf we once took for granted. Variegation may elevate a

A striped or splashed leaf on a common herb can transform it into a showstopper.

simply shaped leaf to a new level of beauty or it may take a beautiful one and make it extraordinary.

Even gardeners who usually enjoy these special leaves may occasionally be turned off by them. Rob's reaction when he first saw a variegated Shasta daisy was: "Icky". An appreciation for variegated foliage is personal. Sometimes the striping or streaking can be unattractive or excessive; sometimes you take a while to develop a fondness for it or discover the secret to showcasing it successfully. Perhaps the contrast between a plant's variegated leaves and its flowers is garish. It takes planning and restraint to use variegated plants to best advantage.

Despite distaste for variegated daisies and a few others, we take pleasure in growing many variegated plants. They provide valuable accents in sunny spots, are almost indispensable in shady ones, and deserve a place in many container plantings.

A striped or splashed leaf on a common herb can transform it into a showstopper and encourage even the most jaded eye to give it a second look. Throughout the alphabet of perennial herbs, gardeners can track down variegated forms: *Artemisia versicolor, A. vulgaris, Astrantia major, Ballota nigra, Calamintha grandiflora, Convallaria majalis, Filipendula ulmaria, Gaura lindheimeri, Hemerocallis fulva, Melissa officinalis, Mentha longifolia, M. suaveolens, Origanum vulgare, Ruta graveolens, Salvia officinalis, Saponaria officinalis, Sedum kamtschaticum, Hylotelephium sieboldii, Teucrium chamaedrys, Veronica longifolia.*

It's worth the search for common perennial herbs that feature eye-catching patterns. The creamy edges of the leaves of *Erysimum linifolium* 'Variegatum' turn this wallflower into the belle of the border. Random cream stripes on the felty gray leaves of lamb's ears are the hallmark of *Stachys byzantina* 'Phantom'. This selection is aptly named because the variegation may be fleeting as the gray reasserts itself; the clump must be monitored.

DAVID COOKS

Several years ago, a reporter's vacation left *The Denver Post* without a cooking column in the middle of the summer. The lifestyle editor asked Rob to fill in with an article on cooking with scented geraniums for summer entertaining—complete with color photograph. Little did she know that Rob's cooking skills are best displayed microwaving popcorn.

But the man is cunning. Rob figured all he would have to do was get me to invent a recipe. After a few moments of panic, I began tearing into every scented geranium on the patio. I'd made pineapple upside-down cake, so I decided that a geranium

upside-down cake was something I could do. I lined a cake pan with parchment and coated the paper with butter. I pressed blanched rose-geranium leaves into the butter, topped them with a half-cup of brown sugar, and filled the pan with a yellow-cake batter.

The geranium leaves made a beautiful pattern on top of the inverted cake and gave it an out-of-this-world flavor. The photograph, taken on the patio with the cake set among pots of scented geraniums, was gorgeous. Rob got the credit, but I got the easy rose-flavored cake recipe, which I still enjoy making. And I get to tell the story.

The white edging on the leaf of the variegated strawberry *Fragaria vesca* 'Albomarginata' gives an already handsome plant new life as a distinctive ground cover. When streaks of yellow decorate the deep green leaves of horseradish (*Armoracia rusticana*), the old plug looks as exciting as a derby winner. The coloration is most prominent in spring and fades as it nears the final summer stretch. Common sage (*Salvia officinalis*) numbers several forms with pretty variegation: 'Purpurascens Variegata' displays dusky purple leaves randomly splashed with pink; 'Tricolor' sports leaves irregularly striped in cream, pink, and dusky purple; and those of 'Icterina' are bright green with gold edges. Differences in golden variegation on sage have led some nurseries to drop the name 'Icterina' and simply lump all the golden ones as 'Variegata', but their effect in the garden is much the same. Both the tricolor and golden forms invite inventive combinations that employ their leaves as foils for contrasting flowers, such as 'Tricolor' with eggplant and purple basil or 'Icterina' with coral bells or red sunroses.

Variegation extends the period of interest of some herbs through the entire season. The yellow-splashed leaves may be simple and small, but the total effect of the variegation lovely, as in *Thymus* × *citriodorus* 'Argenteus'. We like to use mounds of this herb in the front of a border featuring white-flowered and silver-leaved plants such as beach wormwood (*Artemisia stelleriana*) and silver clary (*Salvia argentea*). Variegated lemon thyme (*T.* × *citriodorus* 'Variegatus'), with leaves edged in yellow, is altogether more vibrant than its green counterpart. It makes a pretty skirt for golden-yellow geums or purple bellflowers and echoes the gold of variegated sage.

The gold-edged foliage of *Rosmarinus officinalis* 'Golden Rain' lights up a plant that can seem somber. Another herb whose beauty is enhanced by variegation is comfrey. Dedicated collectors were willing to pay up to $200 for a pot of variegated Russian comfrey (*Symphytum* × *uplandicum* 'Variegatum') when it was offered at a rare plant auction in New York several years ago. Gardeners must still search and be prepared to pay a substantial sum for this cream-edged rarity, which bears the typical pink and blue flowers of the species, but whose leaves constitute its main attraction.

Cream-colored flowers of such plants as Asiatic lilies and daylilies, straw foxglove (*Digitalis lutea*), *Scabiosa ochroleuca,* or *Corydalis ochroleuca* set off their variegated leaves subtly, and they enjoy the same protection from the afternoon sun that keeps the comfrey from scorching. The variegation on the blue leaves of rue may be echoed by a grass, such as the noninvasive form of gardener's garters that grows in clumps, *Phalaris arundinacea* 'Mervyn Feesey'. Grassy, upright foliage appears much bolder when striped with white or cream. Variegated irises, such as *Iris pallida* 'Aurea Variegata' and *I. pseudacorus* 'Variegata', are especially valuable in a garden

In the small space of a window box, variegated scented geraniums complement cascading silver lotus vine and fibrous begonias.

because the foliage makes a contribution long after the flowers have faded. *Acorus gramineus* 'Variegatus' has a similar effect, albeit without the flowers.

The striped ornamental grass *Miscanthus sinensis* 'Morning Light' features a white stripe running down each graceful, slender blade. Yellow stripes cutting across the leaves of *M. s.* 'Zebrinus' provide its common name of zebra grass. Variegated bulbous oat grass (*Arrhenatherum elatius* subsp. *tuberosum* 'Variegatum'), a well-behaved alternative to the free-roaming gardener's garters or ribbon grass, makes an attractive clump that has no intentions of world domination. Variegated society garlic (*Tulbaghia violacea* 'Silver Queen') also makes a stay-put clump in frost-free gardens and is topped by attractive tubular flowers of mauve-pink.

While spiky plants always command attention in the garden, their variegated forms are doubly effective. Classic *Yucca filamentosa* 'Golden Sword' or

the more recent introduction 'Color Guard' provide accents for rue, golden oregano, or the large-leaved form of lamb's ears, 'Helene von Stein' (this cultivar is often sold as 'Big Ears', in an ill-conceived attempt to endear it to the public, but we're resisting the cutesy name).

Variegated New Zealand flax (*Phormium tenax* and *P. colensoi*) form bold clumps in gardens where mild winters don't drop temperatures much below freezing. Some flax are reminiscent of the yuccas, with cream or yellow striping on green leaves, but others are marked with chocolate brown, pink, and salmon. These glow when backlit by the sun.

> **The simple leaves of a honeysuckle take on new importance when they are bright gold with dark green veins.**

A garden can never become monotonous when planted with variegated shrubs and small trees. As specimens or as backdrops, shrubs brighten a scene by injecting a soft, frothy presence. *Cornus alba* 'Elegantissima', with its pale green, white-frosted leaves, brightens a partially shaded garden as if a light had been turned on in a dark room. The blizzard of foliage makes an effective backdrop for flowers of substance, such as those of *Lilium regale* or, later in the season, *Anemone* × *hybrida* 'Honorine Jobert'. Tiny flowers on wispy plants would be lost against such a background.

The yellow-edged leaves of variegated elder (*Sambucus nigra* 'Marginata') commend this attractive shrub for lightly shaded areas. Less vigorous than the plain green or golden forms, it grows much more slowly and rarely reaches more than 6 feet in height. The leaves add interest to the shade garden and accent hostas, brunnera, and lungworts.

The leaves of daphnes are usually nothing to write home about (it's the fragrance of the flowers that inspires sweet poetry)—until, that is, they turn up with a white edge. *Daphne* × *burkwoodii* 'Carol Mackie' forms a rounded mass of thin, dark leaves outlined in cream. Pale pink flowers complete the picture in spring. *D.* 'Briggs Moonlight' is similar but with an important twist—each leaf is cream with a dark green rim. The deep green leaves of *D. odora* 'Aureomarginata' are highlighted with a narrow sliver of white at the margins, accenting the red flower buds as they open on white petals. Of the other shrubs with variegated cultivars, many have traditional herbal uses. These include myrtle, *Weigela*, *Hydrangea*, boxwood, *Kerria*, butterfly bush, maple, *Hebe*, *Aralia*, *Cotoneaster*, *Elaeagnus*, St.-John's-wort, holly, privet, *Pieris*, and blackberry. The list goes on and on.

Vines carry variegated leaves to new heights. The foliage of variegated porcelain vine (*Ampelopsis brevipedunculata* 'Variegata') is irregularly streaked with creamy white and makes an interesting counterpoint to the shiny blue berries. The leaves of variegated Japanese hops (*Humulus japonicus* 'Variegatus') are similarly splashed with streaks and blotches, creating a nice annual accent for a porch trellis or fence. Some gardeners object to its aggressive reseeding, but in our garden—where it behaves as an annual—it self-sows just enough for us to add a few seedlings to containers and give a few away to friends.

The simple leaves of a honeysuckle take on new importance when they are bright gold with dark green veins, as in the case of *Lonicera japonica* 'Goldnet'. Although it would make a bright pattern on a supporting structure, we plant it at the front of a border and let it scamper through lady's mantle and cupid's dart and into a shrub rose. When it occasionally makes a grab for more territory, a couple of quick cuts at the base thwart its spread.

Variegated ivies make more than interesting topiaries. The variegated small-leaved varieties, with patterns in either gold, pale yellow, or white, rarely manage to scale towering heights, but they can be put to use dressing tree trunks and short garden walls or bordering walks. They sparkle in dim light. *Hedera colchica* 'Goldheart' is an aptly named large-leaved ivy that may be used in similar situations for more dramatic results.

Chapter 2

COTTAGE CHIC

COTTAGE GARDENS, stuffed and overflowing with a bounty of herbs, vegetables, and flowers growing in harmony, have timeless appeal. If ever there was a setting made for herbs—aside from an herb garden, that is—it is the cottage garden, or its close kin, the kitchen garden. The cottage-garden tradition has its roots in Europe, especially England, and it predates the great modern push for lawns. It combines informal plantings with informal structure.

Much has been written about the influence of the cottage-garden style on today's gardens. The cottage garden is to horticulture what "country" is to interior design. The deliberate naiveté and lack of pretense are the charms of both "cottage" and "country". As in home decorating, the cottage garden may incorporate influences from France, England, the Southwest, New England, or elsewhere in the choice of plants and colors. Either style—cottage or country—can be overdone, of course, and appear much more affected than the formal styles they were meant to replace. The less gardeners worry about mimicking a quaint cottage look, the more likely they'll achieve an appearance that's unpretentious and truly appealing.

Cottage gardens are personal ones, including favorite flowers, herbs, and even vegetables, and the gardener's personality often pervades them through whimsical touches. They are made to please those who tend them, not to impress the neighbors. Cottage gardens often appear to be a bit overgrown, and we may associate their look with the gardens of our grandparents, many of whom were cottage gardeners long before the term was widely used.

The backdrop to a cottage garden is important, especially when the casual look is introduced to a city yard or a suburb subdivided by fences into square lots. A sense of enclosure—visually screening out the rest of the world and setting the garden apart—contributes to a cottage atmosphere. Many Americans favor the classic picket fence, a friendly divider that invites eyes but not feet. It can be painted or not, fancy or plain. Fences of split rails, adobe, brick, or stone distinguish gardens of different regions. If the fence is made of chain link, it's important to cloak it as quickly as possible to remove all traces of technology. Silver lace vine (*Polygonum aubertii*) will cover a 10-foot span in a single season. It may also engulf elderly people or slow-moving pets. Other perennial vines, such as hops, clematis, or trumpet vine (*Campsis radicans*) take longer to grow to that size, so pop in some seeds of annual morning glories, sweet peas, or scarlet runner beans at the base of the vine. Provide strings or trellis supports along a wooden fence or house to support climbers.

A large cottage garden is quite likely to include fragrant favorites such as mock oranges, lilacs, or old roses, shrubs too large for comfortable accommodation in shallow beds. For height in small cottage gardens,

We eagerly anticipate our visits to Longview Farm in Pennsylvania, where plantswoman Joanna Reed has been gardening for nearly six decades. On this trip, we discovered this raucous combination of cleome, striped canna, plume poppy, dahlias, daphne, silver senecio, and asters.

incorporate clumps of statuesque herbs such as angelica, fennel, sweet Annie, lovage, and broom corn and other grasses. Hollyhocks are the quintessential cottage garden plants. If seed is sown indoors by April, the plants will grow quickly when set out and provide a good show the first year. Hollyhocks are short-lived perennials that are usually at their best the second year.

Other tall plants for the back section include perennial yarrow, monkshood (*Aconitum napellus*), biennial evening prim-rose (*Oenothera biennis*) and annual sunflowers, cleome, castor beans, and cosmos. Plants of more modest height often predominate in cottage gardens, but if something grows a bit too tall, it certainly will do no harm.

Perennials that find favor in a cottage garden include pinks, lady's mantle, coreopsis, daisies, coral bells, Jupiter's beard, blue flax, chives, daylilies, iris, bee balm, and bellflowers. Annuals for fronting small beds include nasturtiums, sweet alyssum, calendula, basil, eggplants, perilla, tomatoes, love-in-a-mist, and bachelor buttons. Those that reseed

Lauren Springer's German four-square garden, above, is more than just a catchall for strawberries, lavender, beans, and flowers for cutting. It's pretty, too. A "scratch 'n sniff" bed, right, includes mint, stock, society garlic, and scented geraniums.

will pop up in different places in following years in time-honored cottage fashion.

A cottage garden is a riot of plants, so bare earth is rarely visible by midsummer. Stuff the plants in closely, cutting down the recommended spacing by at least several inches. In most regions, with the 10- or 12-inch annual spacing suggested by nurseries, you're lucky to achieve a lush look by the first frost. We usually space annuals 6 or 7 inches apart and lop a good 6 inches off the recommended spacing for perennials. Closely planted flowers shade each other's roots, support each other, and suppress the growth of weeds.

In the cottage style, of course, a weed or two can easily be overlooked. No style of gardening is maintenance-free, but cottage

HERBS IN THE GARDEN

gardens allow for a less tidy approach. If the gardener takes a week or two off, there is no shame in having a few plants go to seed. Even one that has flopped to the ground may be less conspicuous.

Cottage gardens reflect the interests of gardeners who like to experiment. Egg-

Overleaf, rustic arbors and a genteel scarecrow guard lavender, borage, alliums, poppies, and baby's breath in the Colorado high country. Above, squash harmonize with nasturtiums and variegated forms of sage and thyme.

plants may consort with roses, or basil with daylilies. The only rule is to throw out the rules. The loose, open style of a cottage garden also makes it an ideal setting for growing bulbs. The withering foliage of spring bulbs is less obtrusive in a cottage garden than it is in a formal border, and the bulbs mature fully but inconspicuously to ensure

an abundant supply of blooms the following spring.

VEGETABLES OUT OF LINE

Both of us come from rural backgrounds. We grew up growing vegetables and a handful of farm-style herbs such as dill and chives. Even in the country, where the emphasis is on production to fill the pantry, freezer, and root cellar with beans, pickles, onions, potatoes, and tomatoes, a love of beauty may flourish. Amid the squash, cabbage, and okra grow irises, peonies, and tough old roses. You can't eat 'em, but they belong. Farm gardens are just cottage gardens without neighbors.

Vegetable gardens were fun when we were young. As adults, we know that they're a lot of work— worth it for tasty tomatoes, beans, and corn that no supermarket can match, but trouble nonetheless. Anyone who grew up on a farm will tell you that vegetables are grown in rows. We used to get out stakes and string to ensure perfectly straight furrows and an equal distance between each plant. If the lettuce didn't come up evenly, we would even transplant the seedlings to make them line up. Rob would have a fit if the neighborhood cats scratched up part of the carrot row.

Instead of consulting a mental-health professional about this obsession, we got over rows. Nothing else in our garden is planted in rows, so why regiment the vegetables? Rows were great for cultivation with horse or tractor, but most backyard vegetable gardens these days aren't even large enough to justify a gas-powered tiller. There's no reason to be stuck in rows.

Relatively small plots that are accessible from all sides keep our vegetable garden weed-free without compacting the soil by

It's no wonder that Victorians waxed poetic over the drooping charms of love-lies-bleeding, paired here with yarrow and cosmos. The two self-sowing annuals can easily compete with the aggressive yarrow.

Herbs in the Garden

DAVID REMEMBERS WHEN

While kids in my hometown spent their summer afternoons at the swimming pool, I was apt to spend mine with my mother and younger siblings in the garden. I learned how to transplant tomatoes before I learned to read, and one of my earliest memories is of planting potatoes. For people who want to get children interested in gardening, I recommend potatoes. The bare foot of a four-year-old is the perfect tool for firming a piece of seed potato into the ground before the furrow is covered. It is also a great lot of fun for a kid.

A wonderful thing about gardening is the many links it provides to the past. The holly at the front of my parents' house came from the neighbor up the road. One iris was from Mother's cousin and another from Dad's older sister. The oak tree came from Grandpa Spittler's woods and the sumac from the river bottom. Grandma Macke planted the pear tree, and Dad set out the apple trees in the first year of his marriage. I still have Aunt Norma's yellow iris and Aunt Ola's big floppy blue one and many other plants that I grew up with.

We didn't have many herbs on the farm, but Rob and I have filled in that gap. Now our home-grown tomatoes taste even better with a little fresh basil, chives, and parsley. I collect fresh poppy seeds for breads and dill for new potatoes. I plant the old standby lettuce varieties that my mother always grew, but now I toss a few leaves of fresh sorrel or arugula into my salads. It's wonderful to grow up and change, but it's also wonderful to grow up and stay the same.

foot traffic. Beds no more than 4 to 6 feet wide allow access to the center for weeding by hand or with a long-handled tool. The ease with which the beds can be dug—which we generally do only to incorporate additional compost —is reason enough to abandon traditional row gardening. Another benefit is not having to deal with a lot of space between rows where weeds can sprout. Some gardeners resort to mulching with newspapers and carpet samples, but that's hardly the look we're after (nor do we stake tomatoes with broom handles or tie up melons with old panty hose).

Rosemary Verey, one of the great British gardeners, was one of the first to demonstrate that vegetable gardens can be beautiful. We've visited her vegetable garden in

Rosemary Verey works magic in her vegetable garden with the humblest of plants.

Barnsley, England, several times and always marvel at its beauty. It lies just across the lane from her ornamental garden, and visitors sometimes have to wait to cross while the cows are driven into the barn for milking. (The plants' robust health leaves no doubt as to the herd's contribution to the garden.)

Rosemary's is no ordinary vegetable plot. Apple trees are trained into the shapes of goblets, and roses grow beside cabbages and strawberries. Salvaged brick and stone have been laid to form geometric paths trimmed in boxwood and filled with patterns of spinach, lettuce, and leeks. Peas and beans climb brush tepees. This practical artistry is food for thought—and, for us, inspiration to seek other ways of designing a kitchen garden.

Another important influence has been Lauren Springer's German foursquare garden. This Colorado plantswoman makes a

A spider with design ideas of its own embroidered a dew-catching web among lettuce and nasturtiums.

utilitarian patch a thing of beauty. Borrowing an easy scheme favored by German immigrants, she divided a sunny area west of her house into four equal squares criss-crossed by grass paths. Smaller beds run along the enclosing picket fence that keeps out the family dogs and separates the foursquare from the more naturalistic plantings on the other side. Within the squares, flowers for cutting mingle with vegetables, herbs, and small fruits such as strawberries. The grass paths make it easy on the knees for planting, weeding, and harvesting.

This freedom of design suits us much better than rows, so we applied the four-square idea to our vegetable plot. We plant in drifts and clumps, considering how the vegetables and herbs will complement one another. Our four-square measures about 20 by 20 feet and we have divided it by brick-edged paths into four equal sections. Where the paths meet in the center, they angle to accommodate a small square for strawberries. Above the strawberries arches a wrought-iron trellis to hold scarlet runner beans and morning glories.

Each of the four beds has a color theme. The purple-and-orange bed is for tomatoes,

eggplant, bronze fennel, pimientos, beets, purple basil, and scarlet opium poppies. The blue-and-yellow section contains corn, dill, cabbage, rue, lettuce, Scotch kale, and gold-leaved forms of oregano, thyme, and feverfew. In the third bed, the accent is on silver and white, with plants such as artichoke, Swiss chard, onions, white eggplant, variegated pineapple mint, thyme, sage, Cuban oregano, and scented geraniums. The fourth bed, with a gray-and-lavender color scheme, holds aromatic lavender, artemisias, catmint, lamb's ears, cardoon, sweet Annie, purple and 'African Blue' basils, lemon mint (*Monarda citriodora*), purple bush beans, arugula, and purple poppies.

The cool-season vegetables such as spinach, lettuce, and beets go in around St. Patrick's Day, but the warm-season tomatoes, corn, and beans don't go in until the frost-free date, which is mid-May in Denver. We stick nasturtiums, marigolds, snapdragons, and zinnias wherever there's a bare spot for a splash of color and for cutting. Filling virtually every inch of space is both an aesthetic decision and a practical one: we weed less and enjoy ourselves more. It's a relief to leave the stakes and string in the potting shed and free ourselves from rigid lines. The vegetable garden used to be a chore; now it's an artistic challenge.

Chapter 3

BOUNDLESS BORDERS

AN ENGLISH-BORN FRIEND who lives in the United States doesn't understand why he sees so few successful borders here. "What's the big deal?" he asks. "You stuff in a bunch of plants." He's right. Many gardeners fuss needlessly about planting borders, and there really is no right or wrong way to design them. When you use plants suitable to the climate, a beautiful border is possible in any part of the country.

Perhaps preconceived notions of what a border should contain get in the way. Certainly there's no point in planting perennials inappropriate to a region, ones that will be toppled by wind, devoured by Japanese beetles, or fried to a crisp. A border can be filled with roses and delphiniums in one region or with yucca and cactus in another. It is the style that defines a border—with plants standing shoulder to shoulder, mingling and mixing—not the specific plants within.

Borders have recently gotten a bad rap in some quarters, viewed by critics as unnatural poor plant habitats because they allegedly subject plants with different cultural needs to the same conditions. Others maintain that borders need to be completely dug up every few years and replanted.

Perhaps some people handle their borders like this, but we don't. We design ours with the cultural requirements of the plants—soil, water, and light—placed first and artistic considerations second. There's no reason why these two viewpoints can't be handled almost simultaneously. When we acquire a new plant, we find out where it comes from and what conditions suit it. That determines where in the garden it goes. Mistakes become apparent quickly. Any high-maintenance plants rarely get preferential treatment and soon go to that great nursery in the sky. Borders evolve through time and need periodic maintenance, but they adapt as well. Our borders are limited only by our imaginations and our climate.

A border can be long, flat, and deep like many classic examples, or it can curve and flow, run up and down hill, and have no formal shape at all. We elected to carve deep, long, symmetrical borders to complement the character of our late Victorian home. The borders run out into the middle of the backyard, breaking up what was once a vast expanse of lawn. Like frames around paintings, the beds provide the structure for the thousands of kinds of plants we grow. They help us organize our collection of plants according to both cultural needs and art. We've fluffed some areas with extra compost and manure to benefit those plants that require richer diets and more water. We have not

The late-season glories of a border spill onto a stone path, with the foliage of rue, thyme, and dianthus providing a calm counterpoint to the fine textures of several salvias including Mexican bush sage, Salvia involucrata 'Bethellii', and Verbena patagonica.

improved other areas, and they receive little if any supplemental moisture.

The entire former front lawn became a single giant border—a borderless border, if you will. It may be viewed from the sidewalk, or the front walk to the door, or the flagstone paths that cut through it. We designed it just as we did the more formal beds, except for placing the tall growth in the middle.

The elements of design are essentially the same whether you're planting a formal border or a borderless border. Many books have been written on the subject of garden design, and most are well worth reading. However, there are just a few basic ideas that

---

The entire former front lawn became a single giant border—a borderless border, if you will.

---

will carry the gardener a long way toward understanding garden design.

For a start, don't be intimidated by the phrase "design principles". The aim of design is simply to create a landscape that is pleasing to the eye. To achieve this goal, plantings should harmonize with their overall setting. A naturalistic planting in conjunction with formal architecture can be just as jolting as a formal border set in the middle of a hayfield.

Using a design appropriate to your home is one key to the successful integration of herbs into your garden. The traditional border can include a huge variety of annual and perennial herbs as well as bulbs with herbal uses. There are useful herbs that can fill all the design functions and provide a heightened sense of enjoyment in the garden. Getting to know plants adds to our appreciation of them. It's an important step in learning how to show them off to their best advantage. Situating herbs in the garden based on cultural requirements

is a must, but after that, the possibilities are nearly infinite.

Color Concerns

Color trends in clothing and interior design sweep across the country every so often, like Technicolor flu epidemics. Harvest gold or avocado appliances transformed nearly every kitchen in the 1960s until austere black and white edged those colors out of vogue two decades later. The psychedelic minis and mint green leisure suits of the 1970s were trundled off to attic trunks when New Age earthy beige replaced them, whereupon a 1990s sea of black drowned out the beige, then. . . ?

Color trends in the garden are rarely as pervasive as those in fashion. A passing fancy for black pansies or iris aside, it seems that gardeners are less susceptible to the latest hype. An individual sense of color is built over time. Some combinations such as blue and yellow or pink and gray never go out of style. On the other hand, gardeners seem more willing in recent years to experiment with richer tones, stronger contrasts, and more cerebral combinations. A direct, violent clash of color such as fuchsia and orange is always dramatic but rarely effective for more than shock value. More subtle variations are easier on the eye and perhaps more pleasing in the long run.

Color is probably the design element that gardeners worry about more than any other, but it offers one of the easiest ways to find interesting combinations of flowers and leaves. Books about color in the garden have been written mostly by English people who have never stood in an American garden in July. Under our umbrella of true-blue, cloudless sky, it is difficult to apply color lessons from those who garden in the pale northern light of cloudy England. Light is variable from region to region, even from garden to garden, and we must all make color decisions largely on our own.

Forget studying the color wheel. It's impossible to subtract green from the garden, so every combination of flower color is

Morning mist hovers above a carefully-planned but casual-looking border in Vancouver that features globe thistle, grasses, baby's breath, cream-flowered Artemisia lactiflora, *and silver* A. *'Powis Castle'.*

based not on how two hues look together, but how they look together with green. Add the variables of alternate leaf colors—bronze, chartreuse, silver, and more—and reliance on classic color-wheel principles of complementary and contrasting colors gets more complicated.

The color wheel is a tool designed for artists who ordinarily work on a relatively small scale. Monet tackled canvases of enormous size, particularly in his famous water

lily series, but even these paintings are small by gardening standards. Certain analogies certainly do exist between painting and gardening, but most painters eventually finish their pieces (gardeners never do) and their works are designed to be viewed indoors, where they are rarely affected by shifting light and shadow, not to mention hail, wind, or grasshoppers.

In the garden, most colors go best with colors of the same intensity. Pastel colors

Herbs in the Garden

harmonize almost effortlessly. A good many garden designers have launched their careers making a lovely pastiche of the pale tones of yellow, pink, lavender, mauve, and blue, like a giant set of Laura Ashley bed linens. Perhaps the most innovative trend of recent years is the investigation of colors that lie outside the pastel safety net. As tones intensify, so does the drama. The pure, undiluted hues of red, orange, blue, purple, and yellow hold their own against one another as well as green. Combinations of these bold colors can be exciting, but many gardeners fear trying their hand at them. This is a pity, for whereas pastels show best in the soft light of dawn and dusk, flamboyant borders with brilliant jewel tones stand up to the bright American sunshine.

Shades in which gray, brown, or black overlies another color, as in a velvety crimson black rose or the skin of a dusky purple eggplant, may seem difficult to work with in the garden. They evoke images of antique Persian rugs, Flemish tapestries, and the paintings of the old masters. We Americans haven't had much experience handling these colors and still feel comfortable with our borrowed English pastels and our own vivid red, white, and blue. But unusual, muted colors such as brick red, burgundy, smoky purple, bronze, terracotta, eggplant, blood red, and dark crimson open up a number of possibilities. They can be contrasted with clear, brilliant colors like pure red or orange, or used to enhance the complex hues of apricot, salmon, or chartreuse. Not every combination is successful, but the ideas continue to flow. Our friend Chris threatens to plant a "bruise border" of lavender, dark red, dusky purple, and greenish yellow. We're taking a wait-and-see attitude.

Our front garden gate opens to a pastiche of bachelor button, coneflower, globe thistle, sea holly, and giant yellow knapweed.

Then there's the single-color border whose best-known example is probably the White Garden at Sissinghurst. It is much more than a white border, of course, since its components include all shades of green and gray. Much livelier and more thought-provoking than almost anyone might have imagined (except perhaps for its creator, Vita Sackville-West), the White Garden has inspired scores of imitations and variations. This horticultural landmark set off a chain reaction of single-color theme gardens and other explorations into using color in unusual ways. Since then, gardens have never been the same.

Not everyone agrees on the merits of its fruit, but few can dislike the blossoms of okra amidst artemisia, plectranthus, and blue Eupatorium coelestinum.

Sissinghurst wasn't built in a day. All of us explore possibilities in our own gardens, one step at a time. One of the best ways to test color combinations is to carry around the garden a flower of a new plant or, better yet, a new plant in flower and try it out alongside other plants in the bed. How does it look? It's a simple test, but it works.

If you have the luxury of planning a new bed or border from scratch, one of the simplest approaches to a color scheme is to begin at one end with soft color combinations and gradually move through the spectrum into bolder hues. We call these "rainbow beds", and they're really difficult to screw up. As an alternative, where space allows, you can segregate color schemes into separate beds, one for soft pastels and another for bolder color combinations. The only people who could mismanage this approach are designers of casino decor in Las Vegas.

We garden writers like to think our ideas are so persuasive that inspired readers will run out, plow under their gardens, and start over from scratch. They don't, of course. An established garden often has constraints that prevent wholesale renova-

tion. Within an existing border, however, it's possible to get tough and make some hard decisions. What works? What doesn't? What has been hanging around since Nixon was in the White House and still has

In a pink, blue, and yellow scheme, cranesbill, lavender, potentilla, and sedum make pleasing companions for roses.

not done much of anything? The best way to invigorate a tired border is to do what writers do—get an editor. Ask a friend whose taste you admire to go through your garden with you to edit out the plants that don't work. Take the best elements and build around them. For example, an existing shrub such as *Rosa glauca* might set the tone for an entire section of border. Edit out the orange daylilies and the golden yarrow, replacing them with mauve, pink, and lavender herb flowers such as stars-of-Persia (*Allium christophii*), pink bee balm, catmint, *Stachys grandiflora,* chives, lavender, and pinks. Introduce drifts of purple sage and bronze fennel for drama and silver artemisia, cardoon, and partridge feather for highlights. As new plants in this color range catch your fancy, and they always do, the scheme will evolve.

Any color scheme carried to its extreme can produce a boring border. There's a wide range of choices for complementing and contrasting flower colors within a given scheme. The critical element is using the right intensity. Strong colors need strong color complements, and subtler shades need equally subtle color complements. The combinations we illustrate here are only points of departure. Just as a musician will improvises on a theme or a cook will tinker with a recipe, a gardener experiments indefinitely.

THE TEXTURAL HERB

Another route to creating interesting pairings is by means of form and texture. Those words have been used so frequently in garden literature that readers' eyes probably blur as they anticipate citations of plants so rare that they grow in only one garden of an isolated castle in northern Scotland. What textural advice boils down to is this: put the big-leaved plants near the little-leaved plants, and put the spiky plants with the roundy-moundy plants. And don't forget to put the fuzzy things with the shiny things.

A bed made up of plants of the same shape and size will be a muddle, no matter how inspired the color scheme. And without contrasts in foliage, no color scheme, however inspired, will pull a garden through. Consider pairing up the bold textures of castor beans, Cuban oregano (*Plectranthus* sp.), and flowering maple (*Abutilon* sp.) with the linear foliage of grasses and irises. In the shade garden, the finely detailed foliage of ferns is a delicate foil for the large heart-shaped leaves of brunnera.

Architectural elements within a traditional border can be reduced to four simple design elements—mats, mounds, sprays, and

We could write a thousand words about contrasts in shape and texture—well, actually, we probably have—but this picture sums it up perfectly. The spears of variegated iris and splattered leaves of Tovara virginica *'Painter's Palette' are balanced by lacy rue, white-edged apple mint, cushions of cranesbill foliage, and flower sprays of* Heuchera *'Palace Purple'.*

spikes. Each of these elements may serve as underpinning or principal feature and may vary in scale from minute to gargantuan. Contrast is the name of the game. Contrast mounds with spikes, add airy sprays, and carpet with mats of ground covers. Vary the scale and texture. Golden oregano, smaller catmints, variegated pineapple mint, and most thymes are low-growing or creeping

plants that can be used at the front of the border as underpinnings for a floral display of taller plants. Creeping veronicas also perform this role well and can soften the hard edge of a border. Larger-leaved ground covers such as wild ginger can offer a significant contrast in texture.

Variation in flower form is another way to create interesting visual effects. Mulleins,

Few perennials match joe-pye weed for autumn dominance in the garden. Its huge flower heads tower above hot pink Agastache barberi *and airy Russian sage.*

foxgloves, nicotiana, and veronicas all provide strong vertical elements, but they are best played against other different forms such as the mounded cranesbills or the frothy, see-through textures of baby's-breath, grasses, or tall verbena (*Verbena patagonica*).

Vines can infuse color into a small area on a wall or freestanding support and provide the strongest vertical elements in a flower bed. A flowering vine such as honeysuckle or clematis is effective as punctuation when it scrambles through a brush tepee, rustic bower, or more formal lattice pyramid. The shape is like a pointed spear of juniper but softer and more interesting. For a lush, overstuffed look, try letting a vine weave itself into an existing vertical plant such as a missile-silo juniper.

Many gardeners are reluctant to include plants that tend to flop. And with good reason: large plants that are prone to late-season spread not only look messy but may also smother their neighbors. Many such plants are programmed to open up late in the season to ensure that their seeds fall away from the mother plant. Some, such as most of the oregano clan, also begin to show new growth in the crown of the plant just as they set seeds. Shearng off the old stalks will clean up the mess while giving the new growth the opportunity it needs to become established.

Other plants are useful in the garden precisely because they do either vine or recline. Nonvining clematis such as *Clematis integrifolia, C. recta, C. stans, C. × durandii,* and *C. heracleifolia,* golden or variegated hops, honeysuckle, morning glories, and poppy mallow (*Callirhoe involucrata*) are just a few plants with the delightful habit of poking up within other plants, helping to create a tightly woven tapestry, the look we like.

> In our garden we maintain a no-bare-earth policy. If by the first of June we have to use a shoehorn to fit another plant in, we're happy.

No Bare Earth

In our garden we maintain a no-bare-earth policy. If by the first of June we have to use a shoehorn to fit another plant in, we're happy. Don't be afraid to let plants touch. Some old-school gardeners surround every plant by expanses of bare earth. Perhaps these are gardeners who have too much time on their hands. Open spaces between plants are an invitation to weeds, and gardeners of this school seem to spend an inordinate amount of time cultivating the soil around their plants.

Constant cultivation is one sure way to keep a plant from reaching its full potential. Most plants send out feeder roots near the surface of the soil, and repeated root pruning stunts them by cutting off their access to water and nutrients and keeping them hungry. Covering open spaces between plants with bark or other nondecomposed mulch is another way to keep plants stunted by starvation. Although these mulches eventually decay and release nitrogen into the soil, the initial stages of decomposition tie up soil nitrogen instead of letting it be taken up and utilized by the plants.

Where torrid summer weather prevails, gardeners often shy away from tight spacing, but their assumption that plenty of space between plants will keep them from rotting doesn't hold water. Plants inappropriate for a climate will rot; the others will do fine. Mediterranean herbs often fall prey to rot and other diseases in the Midwest and South, but other herbs are more suited to a humid climate. Planting Mediterranean herbs in well-drained soil in sloping or raised beds or letting them spill over rocks or gravel paths are strategies for growing these plants in too-humid climates, but they aren't foolproof. Close spacing in a hot climate has the benefit of shading the soil and cooling it to protect the roots. A no-bare-earth policy works in any climate. This may fly in the face of conventional advice that wide spacing improves air circulation, but only electric fans could accomplish that.

ANNUAL ADDITIONS

New gardens need time for perennial plants to reach full size, and there's always an abundance of bare earth for the first year or two. One of the best ways to deal with this problem is to fill the spaces with annuals, but instead of the usual bedding plants sold by the plastic six-pack, try some herbs. Herbal candidates for the new border include nasturtium, borage, castor bean, calendula, Chinese forget-me-not (*Cyno-*

In our campaign to keep our borders overstuffed, we eschew boring bark chips and other fillers. Here thyme and Tuecrium scardonicum *'Crispum' serve as living mulch around bronze sedum, fringed sage, and Mexican fleabane.*

glossum amabile), amaranthus, nicotiana, perilla, dill, fennel, annual salvias, red and yellow orach, viper's bugloss (*Echium vulgare*), opium poppy (*Papaver somniferum*), and many varieties of basil and verbena.

Because most of these annual herbs self-sow, they may become a permanent part of the border. Even as the perennials fulfill

their promise, the annuals will find a way to keep a toehold in the border. This is a good thing because self-sowers can help any design, but few are strong enough to over-power a stalwart perennial.

Annuals also disguise the fading foliage of spring bulbs. Annuals interplanted with bulbs will begin to flourish just as the bulb foliage looks its worst, reducing the temptation to cut it off before it matures.

BORDER CLASSICS

The line between herbal and ornamental gets somewhat blurred when it comes to the classics. Both perennial and annual traditional herbs with handsome good looks are no strangers to herbaceous borders. These are the easily cultivated herbs that have gone mainstream, valued as much for their ornamental properties as for their heritage of usefulness. Success in growing them has encouraged gardeners to integrate other herbs into their borders.

A silver and gold border could easily be built around the classic herbs that have traditionally been incorporated into borders. Winter madness has given Rob a sudden great urge to tear apart an existing border, edit out the colorful bits, and use the remaining plants with silver leaves and/or flowers of gold, yellow, and white to create an homage to the harvest moon. This border would comprise perennials such as lavender cotton, valerian, costmary, elecampane, garlic chives, pearly everlasting, feverfew, Canadian burnet, Jerusalem sage, and every imaginable species of *Artemisia* and *Achillea*. White-flowered forms of coneflower

Herbs on the loose in this classic border include feverfew, pale pink toadflax, and Artemisia *'Valerie Finnis', which invigorate lipstick pink penstemons, maroon* Knautia macedonica, *pink phlox, white and blue bellflowers, purple salvia, and true blue delphiniums.*

*White Japanese anemones get an herbal treatment of purple-leaf sage and Russian
sage in a simple and elegant planting at Joy Creek Nursery in Oregon.*

and lavender would be perfect. A clump of Adam's-needle (*Yucca filamentosa*) could provide a strong vertical accent. Annual sunflowers, marguerite daisies, curry plant, and okra, with its pale yellow hibiscus flowers, would also be good companions in this border.

Alas, as we write this book, snow covers the earth and any chance of digging is months away. The idea will wait.

The classic border herbs, so familiar that we sometimes take them for granted, are

valuable perennials and annuals in any border. Feverfew (*Tanacetum parthenium*) is pretty with almost anything and pairs well with rose campion and nicotiana, but it may be at its best surrounding Asiatic hybrid lilies. This combination looks like a flower arrangement—the roses-with-baby's-breath type of thing that florists have been doing since biblical times, no doubt. A mass of tiny flowers or finely cut leaves surrounding big, showy ones never fails to please. Cultivars of feverfew include 'Golden Ball', 9 inches tall with solid yellow flowers; 'Golden Moss', 6 inches tall with chartreuse leaves and single flowers with white rays and yellow disk; 'White Bonnet' and 'Plenum', 2 feet tall with double white flowers; 'Tom Thumb White Stars', 9 inches tall with white pompons; and 'Snowball', a foot high with double ivory blossoms.

Some people argue that white flowers calm brilliant colors, but the other camp, to which we belong, thinks that white tends to enliven them. Feverfew's mounded, round shape and its flurry of white blooms accent spiky veronica or Jupiter's beard. It's an ideal plant to tie together a pastel grouping of variously shaped plants while bringing out the best in each.

Western gardeners have embraced a Turkish relative of feverfew called snow daisy (*Tanacetum niveum*) for its glorious display of small white daisies above silver-gray foliage. It puts up with heat and drought and thrives as well as feverfew, but if allowed to go to seed, usually dies the second season. We cut most snow daisies down in midsummer to prolong their lives but let a few set seed to keep the line going.

Costmary (*T. balsamita*), also known as alecost or bible leaf, forms a dense, long-lived clump that puts on a late summer show of yellow daisies on stems 3 feet high above flat, wide basal leaves once used as prayer-book markers. *T. b.* var. *tomentosum* looks much like the species but smells strongly of camphor.

Rue (*Ruta graveolens*) works much like feverfew in combinations. The leaves of the species are a delightful shade of blue-green, and they have a fine texture that can showcase blossoms. Some gardeners prefer the Aqua Velva color of the cultivar 'Jackman's Blue'. One favorite companion for rue is rose mallow (*Lavatera trimestris*). The satin sheen of the petals of this old-fashioned annual appear all the more luminescent against the rue leaves. Tweedia (*Oxypetalum*

caeruleum) enhances the grouping. Its unusual turquoise stars complement rue's foliage but don't compete with the rose mallow blooms.

Rue is also superb in combination with the linear shapes of ornamental grasses, especially those that echo its color, such as blue lyme grass or blue fescue. The addition

Deserving of more respect than it gets, lady's bedstraw provides a floral backdrop much like that of lady's mantle for lavender, wood betony, common sage, lamb's ears, and sea pinks in our late June garden.

of variegated kingfisher daisy (*Felicia bergeriana*) and *Plectranthus* 'Wedgwood Blue' is startling. Both are "designer forms" of fairly common plants; kingfisher daisy is a tender annual native to South Africa, while the plectranthus is a tender perennial related to Swedish ivy. Variegated myrtle, variegated sage, and coleus would serve the same function, introducing bolder leaves with yellow edgings to the picture.

Artemisias work the same magic as rue. Their leaves are usually even more finely textured, and most gleam of silver. Our favorite artemisias include the hybrids 'Powis Castle' and 'Huntington', which form luxurious silver clouds that invite adventuresome pairings, such as encircling clumps of *Sedum* 'Autumn Joy', with their red plates of blossoms all the more brilliant against the artemisia's silver threads.

Some people argue that white flowers calm brilliant colors, but the other camp, to which we belong, thinks that white tends to enliven them.

The most effective artemisia combinations come from placing them with vivid flowers or bold leaves. The maroon leaves of 'Blackie' sweet potato at the feet of artemisias knock our socks off, perhaps because the plants blend two passions—bronze with silver. Mix in some other plants with strong character—ornamental peppers, flashy dahlias, or wispy tall verbena—for extra punch.

Dusty miller (*Senecio cineraria*) has a potential far exceeding the standard tasks it is usually assigned, such as edging a bed of geraniums. Judged strictly by its handsome foliage and excellent form, it's worthy of better parts, like a talented actor who gets stuck in B movies. Star dusty miller where it can shine with white nicotiana (also too often taken for granted), Lebanese oregano (*Origanum libanoticum*), white rose campion, or a hundred other candidates. Dusty miller is perennial in frost-free climates and sometimes even in cold winter ones where drainage is excellent. The second summer it produces golden-yellow pompon daisies that must be accounted for in the border's color scheme.

The showy lavender-pink bracts of clary sage (*Salvia sclarea*) complement its broad sage-green leaves. This biennial forms a handsome rosette in its first season and sends up stiff 3- to 4-foot-tall flower stalks the second. Clary sage is a champion of adaptability, performing well in partial shade or full sun in all sorts of soil. If it finds itself too well suited to its location, it can self-seed to a fault.

The larger, more colorful, longer-lived *S. s.* 'Turkestanica' grows up to 6 feet tall and bears lavender-pink blossoms prominently veined in deep pink. It is a lovely, useful border subject. Some writers have attributed its curious nickname, hot housemaid, to its strong scent. Though indeed strong, the scent bears no resemblance to human body odor. To us it's rather like grapefruit. Our friend Angela Overy, who grew up in England, offers another explanation: the flowers' bright pink veins remind her of rosy-cheeked country girls who are often employed at large British estates and are constantly on the run. We prefer Angela's explanation. The aroma can be detected only at close range or when the leaves are crushed.

Perhaps the most beautiful of all the sages, *S. patens,* that deep blue wonder from Mexico, is all the more vivid when placed next to the bright pink daisies of *Aster* 'Alma Potschke' and backed by deep pink obedient plant (*Physostegia virginiana*). It blooms late in the year from seed, but the tuberous roots may be dug and stored over winter in climates where they are unlikely to survive a deep freeze.

Yet another sage, the annual *S. viridis,* has deep purple, pink, or white bracts (the flowers themselves are inconspicuous) that glow vividly when the plant is placed near the front of the border. This species self-sows readily for future seasons. The perennial *S. forskaohlei* sends up 4-foot stalks of violet-blue flowers in June and, if they are cut back by half after flowering, puts on a second show later in the season. Meadow sage (*S. pratensis*), another perennial, bears flowers of lavender-blue, and its flower stalks reach about 3 feet. Its main show is in early summer, when it's a perfect foil for roses.

A stroller past our front fence encounters a dense planting of yarrows, larkspur, white Salvia argentea, *and woolly thyme in the foreground with bellflowers, blue avena grass, catmint, and pink* Phlomis alpina *further back.*

The main attraction of variegated Russian comfrey, Symphytum × uplandicum
*'Variegatum', may be its foliage, but delicate summer flowers also recommend it for inclusion
with sea holly, goat's rue, and delphiniums.*

Although most salvias produce blue, pink, white, or purple flowers, a few species have yellow ones. Some are valuable in frost-free regions, and Jupiter's-distaff (*S. glutinosa*) is hardy to Zone 5.

Any number of beautiful perennial sages may be found in specialist's catalogs and are easily grown from seed. Many hold special appeal to gardeners in the western states because they often exhibit good tolerance to heat, drought, and even deer.

Gardeners in the South and on the East Coast have a field day with sages from tropical and subtropical regions. These often flower late in the season and, north of New York City and Philadelphia, may get nipped by frost in their prime. *S. guaranitica* is deep ultramarine blue; the cultivar 'Black and

Blue' has nearly black bracts that intensify its dramatic qualities. It grows up to 6 feet tall. *S. involucrata* 'Bethellii' is rose-pink with plump buds reminiscent of those of turtlehead (*Chelone obliqua*). It also grows up to 6 feet tall. *S. vanhouttei* looks much like the scarlet bedding annual, *S. splendens*, but it is taller (up to 3 feet), and its flowers are maroon red. We tried to grow it one year but didn't manage to get it into bloom before the first snowfall, so now we're content to admire it during autumn trips to mid-Atlantic and southern states.

Herb gardeners from northern states envy those in the South who have no trouble getting pineapple sage (*S. elegans*) to bloom before frost. As a border plant in the South, its brilliant red tubular blooms make a spirited show with late-blooming Mexican bush sage (*S. leucantha*), asters, cannas, and ornamental grasses.

Among the most beautiful of all herbs are the purple coneflowers (*Echinacea* spp.), some of which have become a staple in both the medicine cabinet and the border. The best-known species, *E. purpurea*, features a bristly orange and brown cone and distinctive lavender-pink ray florets. Breeding has raised these petals from a drooping position to a perky horizontal one, but the flower is lovely in either pose. The ray flowers don't fall from the flowers when they fade, but linger to curl and bleach for winter interest. Many cultivars have been selected for height from 2 to 4 feet and the intensity of their pink coloration. Creamy white cultivars like 'White Swan' expand the options for artistic uses.

The echinacea species most esteemed for its ability to stimulate the immune system is *E. angustifolia*. It grows to about 2 feet in height and has narrow, spear-shaped leaves and flowers with rose-purple rays. *E. pallida* is similar but taller and wider. Tennessee coneflower (*E. tennesseensis*), an endangered species that several nurseries now propagate, has dark green, lance-shaped leaves and pink flowers with green cones.

Perhaps because yarrows grow so readily and reliably, at least in dry climates, some people look down their noses at them. Those who prefer plants that are rare and difficult to grow should just skip the genus *Achillea* altogether, for it is full of great, nearly foolproof border perennials. Topping our list are cultivars derived principally from *A. filipendulina,* such as mustard yellow 'Coronation Gold', bright yellow 'Gold Plate', and golden yellow 'Parker's Variety'. Granted, these robust, brilliant cultivars eas-

---

Judged strictly by its handsome foliage and excellent form, dusty miller is worthy of better parts, like a talented actor who gets stuck in B movies.

---

ily overwhelm a delicate pastel theme, but their height (3 to 4 feet), attractive ferny, sage-green foliage, and bold show of dense, flat-headed flower clusters recommend them. Suitable companions with these golden yarrows include the purple flowers of *Campanula glomerata* 'Joan Elliot' and *Salvia × superba* 'May Night'. These yarrows also serve as brilliant anchors in a "harvest moon" border with all manner of silver foliage and yellow, white, and cream flowers.

Woolly milfoil (*A. tomentosa*) also displays golden yellow blossoms, but they are held just 6 inches above its low mat of gray-green woolly leaves. It grows best in a sunny, well-drained spot, as do most of the other yarrows. *A. × lewisii* 'King Edward', grows to about 10 inches; this pretty spreading plant has gray foliage and pale yellow blossoms. It looks like a miniature form of the classic 'Moonshine', and indeed they share a parent, *A. clypeolata*. Just 2 feet tall, 'Moonshine' would seemingly deserve a place in any planting where pastels rule, but like many of this genus, it is susceptible to leaf diseases in hot, humid climates. With even paler flowers the color of butter, and foliage even more silver, the cultivar 'Anthea' is as useful as 'Moonshine' in borders or for cutting and drying.

A daring color scheme at Bella Madroña, the garden of Jeof Beasley and Jim Sampson in Oregon, is highlighted by a bronze-leaf banana, maroon-red amaranth, coral Jupiter's beard, Phygelius capensis, *and a surprise gazing ball nearly hidden in its iron chamber.*

Some yarrows should be viewed with suspicion because of their invasiveness. *A. millefolium* can rapidly spread out of control in moist, rich soil. Although its white or pale pink flowers have their charms, selected varieties are much prettier and behave somewhat better, but we grow them lean and mean to keep them in bounds. Their names describe them well: 'Cerise Queen',

'Lavender Lady', 'Paprika', 'Fire King', and 'White Beauty'. 'Summer Pastels' come in a variety of subtle shades ranging from buff pink, salmon, and apricot to pale yellow. Sneezewort (*A. ptarmica*) has narrow, glossy green leaves with little white flowers like those of feverfew on spindly stems up to almost 2 feet tall. The best of the selections from this species has long been 'The Pearl', with double white flowers. 'Improved Pearl', a recent introduction, is more compact, and thus less likely to flop. Heat and drought-loving Kellerer's yarrow (*A.* × *kellereri*) blooms throughout much of the summer with white flowers on 8-inch stems above unusual strap-shaped silver leaves.

The main drawback to growing bee balm, also known as Oswego tea, is its susceptibility to powdery mildew. Most forms of *Monarda didyma* attract mildew like a magnet, but some new cultivars are more resistant. A recent introduction, rose-pink 'Marshall's Delight', appears to deliver on its promise of mildew-free leaves in your cup of Oswego tea. We rarely have a mildew problem with 'Croftway Pink' or the hybrids that involve *M. fistulosa*, such as 'Violet Queen' and 'Prairie Night', but not every gardener can make that claim. (Our excuse for mildew, if a visitor is rude enough to point it out, is that the plant in question is a rare silver-leaf form.)

Two species of *Monarda* with no propensity for mildew are lemon mint (*M. citriodora*) and horsemint (*M. punctata*). The former is grown as an annual in northerly climes and reaches about 3 feet with whorls of flowers characteristic of the genus displayed along the top two-thirds of the stems. The color is an attractive deep mauve pink, and it's possible to select for the richest tones over several seasons by weeding out the palest-flowered plants.

Horsemint's flowers of yellow and white speckled with pink complement bright green leaves that smell strongly of mint and camphor. This plant also grows about 3 feet tall and is beautiful enough to include in the garden whether or not it's needed to make an equine liniment.

Other classics that provide good textures and colors in a border are *Santolina*, including the green-leaved *S. rosmarinifolia* and the woolly, gray-leaved lavender cotton *S. chamaecyparissus*. Both species are traditionally used in knot gardens and are sheared regularly to remove the buttons of yellow flowers that otherwise rise on wiry stems above the summer foliage. Several cultivars of lavender cotton are compact, with dense, silver foliage; they include 'Nana', about 6 inches high, and 'Pretty Carol', 10 to 15 inches tall. 'Lemon Queen' grows about as tall as the latter but, despite its name, produces buttermilk-yellow blossoms that give the plant a softer look.

English lavender (*Lavandula angustifolia*) is one of a few species of lavender that survives the rigors of winter below Zone 6. A pretty, useful plant in many ways, its best-known cultivars are the lavender-blue 'Munstead' and the deeper violet-blue 'Hidcote Blue'. Pink forms include pale 'Rosea', 'Hidcote Pink', and true pink 'Miss Katherine'.

For gardeners who have trouble overwintering English lavender because of wet soil, the lavandins (*L. × intermedia*, including hybrids between *L. angustifolia* and *L. latifolia*) are useful because they can take more moisture and are almost as hardy as English lavender. Fragrant, light purple 'Provence' comes from the French countryside where it is widely grown for its flowers and oil. 'Grosso' is another French cultivar with showy, deep purple flower heads. 'Alba' sports white flowers that complement its gray leaves. It really lights up a planting. We also like robust lavender-blue 'Grappenhill' and rosy-purple 'Twickel Purple', whose foliage takes on a purple cast in winter.

*The beauty of saffron crocus, which may be diminished when viewed against bare soil, comes to full flower when set against the finely-cut leaves of aptly-named partridge feather (*Tanacetum densum *var.* amani*).*

The West Coast, with a climate like that of the Mediterranean region, is true lavender country and ideally suited to growing several species that don't make it in other parts of the country. One is stick-a-dove lavender (*L. stoechas*), which acquired its whimsical name from the featherlike bracts poking out of the top of the flower heads. Another folk name is Spanish butterfly. This small shrub has needlelike gray-green leaves and wiry stems topped by the purple "feathers", and it blooms from spring through much of the summer if regularly deadheaded. The foliage of fringed lavender (*L. dentata*) is deep green with deeply indented edges. Its flowers are a light shade of lavender-blue. By contrast, *L. multifida*'s leaves are finely dissected and its flowers are small and bluish-purple.

Similar to lavender in its use in the garden is vervain (*Verbena officinalis*) with wiry stems from 2 to 3 feet in height and tiny lavender-blue flowers. This neglected perennial deserves a second look. Goat's rue (*Galega officinalis*) has also fallen from favor, although it was once considered an almost indispensable feature of any proper border. It makes a grand show in early summer, growing up to 5 feet tall or more with masses of softly tinted lavender flowers that resemble those of peas. The white form is equally pretty. Once used in folk medicine to increase milk flow, this perennial grows easily in moist, well-drained soil and suffers few ailments.

Alkanet (*Anchusa azurea*) also gets short shrift from most modern garden designers. It's a short-lived perennial whose root has been used in cosmetics but whose great attraction is its masses of small, five-petaled true blue flowers that appear in early summer and sometimes rebloom if the 5-foot stems are cut down after flowering. The broad, hairy green leaves cover quite an expanse, so there's a hard-to-disguise vacancy in the back of the border after they're gone, which may explain the current lack of enthusiasm for alkanet. It can be invasive if grown in rich soil.

Valerian (*Valeriana officinalis*) also ensures its survival with a megacrop of seedlings, but its good-looking leaves and sweet, pink-tinged white flowers may be worth the effort. As the seedlings emerge in spring, we select those with the deepest bronze color and weed out the rest. As a result, we've developed a stable population whose leaves make an effective backdrop for tulips and daffodils (although the foliage changes to green as summer arrives). Jupiter's beard (*Centranthus ruber,* but often called red valerian) also reseeds too well for tidy gardeners. England seems to have forgiven the plant its prodigious ways, and we may as well do the same. Jupiter's beard looks dramatic clinging to a seemingly impossible toehold in an ancient castle wall—or any other wall, for that matter. The most common flower color is a deep pink, but cultivars of bronze red, medium pink, and white are available. And who knows what color a self-sown seedling may reveal?

The spires of Canadian burnet (Sanguisorba canadensis) rise like a six-foot sculpture of bottle brushes in autumn, begging for inclusion in a border with other late season behemoths like joe-pye weed and asters.

AUTUMN IN THE BORDER

The contribution of herbs to the landscape can continue into autumn. Late bloomers combine with plants displaying fruit or pods from earlier flowering, not to mention colorful fall foliage. Gardeners often face the end of the season with mixed emotions. For some, the first frost comes as a relief, wiping out the mistakes and putting an end to a season of struggles and frustrations. For others, autumn is a giddy last fling. They loosen up, relax their rigid garden grooming habits, and allow the plants to do their own thing.

Like last call at a singles bar, late-blooming flowers take advantage of fewer competitors to attract pollinators. Seed heads ripen, break open, and release their contents to the wind. Many leaves trade their green pigments for gaudier colors, while fruit and berries mature and fall to earth. Tidiness freaks rake leaves and chop plants to the ground in an odd ritual called "putting the garden to bed" that seems the exact opposite of the autumn fruitfulness that nature intends. Those of us who have overcome these habits merely sit back and enjoy the show.

Perennial herbs that flower late command notice. The fluffy white flowers of Canadian burnet (*Sanguisorba canadensis*) look like white bottlebrushes. They can reach 6 feet tall above toothed, divided leaves, making this an outstanding specimen in the autumn border. Joe-pye weed (*Eupatorium purpureum*) makes an even more dramatic focal point (up to 12 feet tall in moist soil) with its rounded heads of mauve pink. Few gardens need more than one plant. The relatively compact 'Gateway', at just 6 feet tall, may be more suitable for gardeners with limited space. White flowers set the cultivar 'Bartered Bride' apart. Boneset (*E. perfoliatum*) blooms from late summer into fall with large heads of white flowers on 5-foot stalks and crinkled, lance-shaped leaves. It thrives in a damp spot. Also valued for their late bloom are the much shorter pearly everlasting (*Anaphalis triplinervis* and *A. margaritacea*), with heads of chalky-white flowers above thin silver leaves.

> Among the most beautiful of all herbs are the purple coneflowers (*Echinacea* spp.), some of which have become a staple in both the medicine cabinet and the border.

DAVID ON THE OFF-SEASON

Denver gardeners have a secret weapon in their gardening arsenal—winter. Situated at the junction of the mountains and the plains, Denver has a climate similar in many ways to the steppes of Russia and Turkey. Winters are cold and very dry (although much of our average scant 14 inches of rainfall comes as snow). Many Mediterranean herbs, bulbs, and grasses are perfectly suited to our dry winters.

After the first killing frost, Rob and I try to pull and dispose of most of the annuals left standing, but we leave our perennials just as the frost found them. Even in the dead of winter, they recall the colors and combinations of bloom. In wetter climates, gardens can turn to mush if left to stand through the winter, but Denver garden cleanup can wait until those warm, sunny days in January or February when we have cabin fever. Then we can cut back the old garden and think about the coming of spring.

It's worth the effort to compose parts of the garden with an autumn theme, such as in this well-orchestrated planting of joe-pye weed, Roman wormwood, Russian sage, and the burnished spikes of acanthus.

Contrasting with the fiery foliage colors of the season are the airy lavender panicles of Russian sage (a *Perovskia atriplicifolia* hybrid). This splendid perennial tolerates a broad range of climates and conditions. Garlic chives (*Allium tuberosum*) also thrive in a wide range of circumstances, their alabaster white flowers all the more welcome late in the season in the company of artemisias and horehounds.

Late-blooming oreganos such as *Origanum laevigatum* 'Hopleys' and 'Herrenhausen' soften the border with multitudes of pink-violet blossoms, very effective with gray santolina and lavender. A similar airy effect is achieved by planting lesser catmint (*Calamintha nepeta*) for its masses of tiny blue blossoms. We combine it with the plum-red leaves of *Heuchera* 'Royal Knight', santolina, and the bright pink double meadow saffron *Colchicum autumnale* 'Waterlily'.

The most anticipated fall bloom for most gardeners who cook is saffron crocus (*Crocus sativus*), whose purple-striped lavender goblets open to reveal the three valuable red stamens. We carefully pick the stamens from our small but reliable patch that thrives along a heat-trapping flagstone path where the plants receive little extra irrigation. We chose the hottest, most inhospitable spot we could find, the better to simulate conditions of the Middle East and Spain where saffron crocus is commercially cultivated. Thyme and partridge feather (*Tanacetum densum* var. *amani*) also enjoy these conditions, and the saffron flowers poke up prettily through their low mounds of leaves.

One of the most delightful aspects of autumn—for gardeners as well as wildlife—is the profusion of fruits. Strolling beneath our grape arbors, we inhale the sweet perfume of ripening fruit and perhaps pluck a handful or two of tart 'Concord' or sweet

We'd miss the freeze-dried beauty of the late autumn garden if we took the weed-whacker to the seed heads of purple coneflower, sedum, and pearly everlasting.

'Niagara' grapes. Apples falling from our ancient tree litter the brick path through the shade garden. Squirrels nibble a few of them, but they are too stuffed to put much of a dent in the crop. A sprinkling of scarlet hips begins to appear among the shrub roses. The showiest hips are found on seaside rose (*Rosa rugosa*), dog rose (*R. canina*), sweetbriar (*R. rubiginosa*), apothecaries' rose (*R. gallica* 'Officinalis') and Cherokee rose (*R. laevigata*).

The bright red fruits of dogwood look like heads of miniature maces, the medieval clubs used to crush armor, or perhaps warty maraschino cherries. The inky purple fruit of pokeberry (*Phytolacca americana*) appear as the leaves turn to red and purple. A Chinese species, *P. clavigera,* has showy pink flowers followed by dark purple berries on red autumn stems with yellow foliage. Unfortunately, it is hardy only to Zone 6. The drying pods of blackberry lily (*Belamcanda chinensis*) burst open to reveal rows of seeds like polished onyx.

In cottage and vegetable gardens, maturing gourds, pumpkins, and squash intertwine with asters, mums, amaranths, sweet Annie, nasturtiums, and showstoppers such as lion's ear (*Leonotis leonurus*), whose whorls of flowers rise on 5-foot stems and appear to have been cut from orange felt.

Throughout the rest of the garden, seed heads of milkweed, coneflowers, rudbeckias, sunflowers, dill, fennel, poppies, yucca, hyssop, and liatris attract birds that amuse us with their antics. Herbs with bright autumn tints include herb Robert (*Geranium robertianum*) and other cranesbills, strawberries, sumac, lemon grass, and feathery *Amsonia hubrectii,* which is at its best in autumn when its thin leaves turn yellow. We continue to appreciate the gray foliage of lamb's ears, artemisias, and lavenders as cool companions to the autumn stars such as Japanese anemone, asters, turtlehead, obedient plant, and 'Autumn Joy' sedum.

We've come to value plants in all stages of their life cycles, from emergence to flowering to fruiting. Cold northerly winds may bring a bit of melancholy, but there is much to celebrate in the autumn garden.

Chapter 4

SHADE AND STREAM

THE HERBS THAT pervade our cooking are nearly all native to the sun-splashed Mediterranean region. Those from woodland and wet environments receive scant attention—and that's too bad. Moist, shady gardens suit a surprising number of herbs that are often overlooked, including beautiful woodland perennials and shrubs. These lovely though somewhat unassuming plants come from wooded areas around the globe, and Americans have the opportunity to provide homes for all of them.

The plants of our own forests link us to the herbal traditions of native Americans, some of which were adopted early on by European settlers. Several American woodland herbs have made it into mainstream gardens. Bloodroot (*Sanguinaria canadensis*), mayapple (*Podophyllum peltatum*), and jack-in-the-pulpit (*Arisaema triphyllum*) herald spring in many shade gardens, perhaps because people treasure their childhood memories of discovering these charmers in the woods.

MEET THE NATIVES

As the spring sun bathes the forest floor through a web of bare branches, the first shoots emerge from the crumbly, black soil formed from years of autumn leaf mold. Many woodland plants take advantage of this brief sunny period to bloom and set seed. Some disappear within weeks after the trees leaf out, while others expand their leaves to catch as much light as possible through the green canopy.

Few of these plants can compete with the floral fireworks of sunny meadow flowers, but many possess an unrivaled grace and charm. Shade gardens, as we create them around our homes, reflect a different sensibility from those that we plant in sun. Gone are the neon colors, the flamboyance, and the showmanship. Here there is a softer palette, plus sophistication and subtlety. We appreciate our shade garden throughout the seasons almost as an antidote to the brilliance of the sunny garden. In the heat of summer, it's a refuge that cools and refreshes.

The first signs of spring arrive as a flurry of snowdrops underfoot and a scattering of yellow stars on the branches of the native witch hazel (*Hamamelis vernus*). American herbs such as bloodroot, trillium, jack-in-the-pulpit, and mayapple bloom among daffodils and other imports. They are followed by many beauties native to moist, rich woods. It's an extensive, varied lineup: trout lily (*Erythronium americanum*), partridgeberry (*Mitchella repens*), red trillium (*Trillium erectum*), round-lobed hepaticas (*Hepatica americana* and *H. acutiloba*), wood betony (*Pedicularis canadensis*), columbine (*Aquilegia canadensis*), wild geranium (*Geranium maculatum*), Solomon's seal (*Polygonatum* spp.), dwarf crested iris (*Iris cristata*),

An old pump sets the stage for a damp planting of lady's mantle, ferns, and hostas.

A perennial favorite (even though it's strictly a biennial), foxglove shows to advantage in our shade garden beneath the sizable umbrellas of giant cow parsnip (Heracleum mantegazzianum).

spikenard (*Aralia racemosa*), Jacob's ladder (*Polemonium reptans*), rue anemone (*Anemonella thalictroides*), Dutchman's breeches (*Dicentra cucullaria*), and bunchberry (*Cornus canadensis*).

Shady herbs that we grow primarily for their attractive foliage include wild ginger (*Asarum canadense*), maidenhair fern (*Adiantum pedatum*), male fern (*Dryopteris filixmas*), alumroot (*Heuchera americana*), and wild yam (*Dioscorea villosa*).

Small shrubs that display spring flowers include wintergreen (*Gaultheria procumbens*), hollies (*Ilex* spp.), and grape hollies (*Mahonia aquifolium* and *M. repens*). The yellow flowers of grape holly are especially effective against last year's leathery maroon-brown leaves. For open woods, small, showy spring-flowering trees or shrubs include flowering dogwood (*Cornus florida*), redbud (*Cercis canadensis*), and great rhododendron (*Rhododendron maximum*). Small trees for dry, open woods are fringe tree (*Chionanthus virginicus*) and sassafras (*Sassafras albidum*). We marvel at the adaptability of Carolina allspice (*Calycanthus floridus*), native from Virginia to Florida but hardy to at least Zone 5. Its odd flowers that look a bit like purple-brown mums have an intriguing odor that reminds us of cloves steeped in shaving lotion.

Many viburnums, especially *Viburnum* × *burkwoodii* and *V.* × *rhytidophylloides* 'Alleghany', also entice the nose with sweet spicy scents. They thrive in partial shade and often benefit from being positioned in a spot sheltered from wind. The clovelike fragrance of 'buffalo' currant (*Ribes odaratum*) and yellow currant (*Ribes aureum*) also

*We eagerly await the spring appearance of double-flowering bloodroot (*Sanguinaria canadensis '*Multiplex'*) in our shade garden, even though we ordinarily frown on many double forms of otherwise single blossoms.*

recommends them for inclusion in a garden with partial shade.

Throughout the season, we appreciate the fine-textured, deep green foliage of hemlocks (*Thuja* spp.) and the weeping form of Alaska cedar (*Chamaecyparis nootkatensis*). In our area, both must be positioned to protect them from winter wind and sun. A weeping Alaska cedar doesn't suit everyone. Ours was one of a trio our friend Tom planted in a garden he'd designed. The owner couldn't stand the cedars, claiming they reminded her of the three witches in *Macbeth*. We'd

have gladly found a home for the entire coven, but the woman had already axed two by the time Tom disarmed her. "Methinks she doth possess one taco less than a combination platter," poor Tom observed.

SPRING TREASURES

Americans have just begun to discover how easy the primroses, long beloved in Europe, are to grow. Oxlip (*Primula elatior*), cowslip (*P. veris*), and English primrose (*P. vulgaris*) do best in moist, humus-rich soil across most of the northern tier of states. As long as they are not allowed to dry out, the species survive the heat of summer far better than the more colorful hybrids. Drumstick primrose (*P. denticulata*) from the Himalayas is also remarkably easy to grow and long-lived, sending up round, tightly packed flower heads in lavender, mauve-pink, or white. Because they're almost too eager to bloom in early spring, the flowers often get frozen by late arctic spells.

Leopard's bane (*Doronicum orientale*) seems to have kept Europe free of leopards in days past and may be irrelevant today. But its golden yellow daisies—so unexpected in the shade and so early in the year—recommend leopard's bane whether there's a predator on the prowl or not. Good companions include the yellow archangel *Lamium galeobdolon* 'Hermann's Pride', which blooms at the same time, its pale yellow flowers studding upright stems with silver-marked green leaves; sweet violets of purple or white; and *Valeriana phu* 'Aureum', which echoes the daisies with its yellow-tinted leaves. Another classic companion are the airy blue sprays of heartleaf (*Brunnera macrophylla*), or Siberian bugloss.

Two carrot-family members with ferny foliage, chervil (*Anthriscus cerefolium*) and sweet cicely (*Myrrhis odorata*), thrive in the cool, moist weather of spring. Chervil, a hardy annual, sends up an umbel of tiny white flowers on a short stalk. As seeds set, the finely cut leaves die a pink-tinted death. Sweet cicely grows 2 to 3 feet tall, forming a graceful mound of shiny, finely dissected leaves topped by white flower heads—like a compact Queen Anne's lace. We like it paired in partial shade with broad-leaved ornamental rhubarb (*Rheum palmatum*) or purple-flowered honesty (*Lunaria annua*) and forget-me-nots at its feet.

Moist, shady gardens suit a surprising number of often-overlooked herbs, including beautiful woodland perennials and shrubs.

Herb Robert (*Geranium robertianum*) has its fans and detractors. Overshadowed by its showier cranesbill relatives, humble herb Robert is valued for its aromatic foliage that forms short mounds about 8 inches tall with small, deep pink blossoms. It seeds too well for some gardeners' taste and has become a regular pest in parts of the Pacific Northwest. Successful even in dry shade, herb Robert makes a fine show with divided leaves that turn crimson even before fall arrives. Colonies of seedlings often find ideal spots for themselves, mingling harmoniously with yellow-flowered St.-John's-wort, the cinnamon red flowers of *Trillium sessile*, and blue-leaved *Hosta sieboldiana*.

Though too aggressive for a small space, sweet woodruff (*Galium odoratum*) with its colonizing ways is a natural for difficult partial-shade situations. Its small white late-spring blossoms complement those of deciduous shrubs such as lilacs, viburnums, or hydrangeas. The fine texture of both its prolific flowers and tiny leaves are an admirable backdrop for wood hyacinths and daffodils in spring or colchicums in autumn.

Foxglove (*Digitalis purpurea*) continues to enchant gardeners with its spikes of tubular bells and its mystique. Who doesn't want to believe that the spots inside foxglove flowers were left by fairies, or that the sly fox put the flowers on his feet in order to sneak quietly into the henhouse? Another explanation is that the plant was originally called fox *gleow*—a gleow being a northern European musical instrument of bells. To buy this version, of course, it's necessary to believe that a fox can display musical talent.

Who cares? Foxgloves are beloved by almost every shade gardener. Besides the familiar pink and rose-violet blossoms, foxgloves are also available in white, apricot, and pale yellow. These strains must be grown in isolation to keep them pure. Foxgloves self-seed with abandon in moist areas and are naturalized in many places to the point of becoming weeds. Alas, they rarely self-sow for us because they drop their seeds in midsummer, the driest time in our garden.

Enjoying their late spring show (which we like to imagine is enjoyed by musically inclined neighborhood pets), we collect our foxglove seed and sow it in flats in a shady spot. We prick out the seedlings, pot them up, keep them moist through the summer, and transplant them to the garden in late summer or early autumn. We keep fertilizer to a minimum since we've found that big, lush plants often succumb over winter but the runts are almost always the ones that make it through.

SUMMER IN THE WOODS

Many gardeners lament the lack of summer color in the shade garden and plant masses of begonias, impatiens, and coleus. Though beautiful in their own right, these tropical plants appear distinctly out of place in a naturalistic garden. We use them sparingly in strategically placed pots in shady

ROB PONDERS THE POND

Our goldfish pond has been a great pleasure. We built it one afternoon from 4 × 4's, digging down about a foot and then raising the lip about 3 feet above ground level. Some plants float on the surface; others grow in pots that are either submerged or sunk to their rims on top of concrete support blocks.

We've resisted the temptation to bond with our goldfish. Most arrived unceremoniously in a plastic bucket from our friend Tom's overpopulated pond, and other friends have brought by a few special fish with showy white markings. We treat them all the same, with benign neglect, but they have us fairly well trained to scatter flakes of food when they come to the surface to beg.

A pump keeps the water circulating and runs a trickling fountain head. Several times during the summer, we pull out the pump and clean the algae that threatens to clog it. Snails and oxygenating plants help keep the pond clean enough to support the fish. Birds like to drink from the pond, and we've also provided them with a bowl of fresh water on the edge of the pond. We often spot robins bathing ecstatically in it.

It wasn't too much work for the plea-sure that the pond gives us. Besides the soothing sound of trickling water and the amusement of watching the fish dart about, we enjoy the aquatic plants—water lilies, papyrus, water cannas, elephant's-ear, and rushes. When winter arrives, we move the tropical plants to the basement, unplug the pump, and stop feeding the fish. Ice covers the pond's surface through much of the winter. When the big thaw eventually comes, we worry that our fish will have turned into fish sticks, but they always make it through. So we bring out the plants and start all over again.

We've only had one problem. I woke up one morning and headed for the patio to read the paper and feed the fish. The pond was a mess—it looked like it had been mugged. The fountain head and plants had been knocked off their supports, and potted plants on the edge had been knocked in. Water hyacinths were strewn around the patio. Raccoons had discovered a brand-new restaurant. They're not usually encountered in the middle of the city, but our corn was just ripening at the time, so it made a nice side dish to their seafood dinner.

A shady, almost-neglected corner is populated by a hardy band of no-fuss herbs including Solomon's seal, lamb's ears, lungwort, grape hyacinths, iris, and bergenia.

areas but resist the temptation to implement Butchart Gardens–style bedding as replacement for those graceful denizens of spring, the trout lilies, primroses, and trilliums. It would be like following a Judy Collins folk song by an extravaganza from the Radio City Music Hall Rockettes. There's a place for both, but not on the same stage.

We respect the summer serenity of our woodland garden, but that doesn't mean it's devoid of floral interest. The glowing golden blossoms of St.-John's-wort (*Hypericum calycinum*) beg us to examine their centers of fiber-optic filaments. Although St.-John's-wort performs equally well in a sunny location, we grow it where its evergreen leaves are protected from winter sun and wind.

More yellow blossoms light up the shade when celandine poppy (*Chelidonium majus*) blooms in early summer above handsome gray-green leaves that never show any slug damage. The four-petaled yellow flowers are slightly smaller than a quarter but appear in clusters and may repeat if the 3-foot stems are cut back after flowering. The plant is sometimes called poor man's iodine since its golden-orange sap reputedly relieves itching from insect bites. When we cut it back to help curb its self-seeding, our hands and arms become stained with the sap. We inherited our celandine poppies when we bought the place. They grew in concert with poison hemlock (*Conium maculatum*) and bouncing Bet (*Saponaria officinalis*) beneath an ancient apple tree clinging to the banks of the irrigation ditch. We've made small attempts to civilize the area, but we don't have the heart to exterminate the plants that colonized the property a century before we came along. Besides, if the old pipes in our house burst we could head down to the ditch, work up a nice lather from the saponaria, dress our mosquito bites with the golden iodine, and end it all with the hemlock when we get the plumber's bill.

In more refined areas of the shade garden, we grow a number of decorative herbs for summer interest. These include the perennial wood alkanet (*Pentaglottis semper-*

A calmer, quieter design prevails beneath trees. Not a flower is to be seen in midsummer, but the harmonious relationship between Pulmonaria *'Roy Davidson', lamium, ivy, Jacob's ladder, and tiarella is still evident.*

virens), with coarse, broad leaves and frothy, foot-high sprays of pale blue flowers, anise (*Pimpinella anisum*), a 2-foot annual with ferny leaves and umbels of white flowers, and purple plantain (*Plantago major* 'Rubrifolia'), with plum-purple foliage that we appreciate springing up around the dining patio even though we fight the common green form in the lawn. Its dark rosettes are a pleasing counterpart for the tumbling mounds of self-heal (*Prunella vulgaris*), which send up short spikes with purple, lilac, or white flowers. Cut-leaf prunella (*P. webbiana*) features darker leaves tinted with purple and rosy-purple blossoms.

We value the true blue flowers of Jacob's ladder (*Polemonium caeruleum*) and its shorter, almost-creeping cousin *P. reptans*, sometimes called by the unsavory name of abscess root. We're especially excited about 'Lambrook Mauve', a cultivar of the latter that Rob brought back from England. Arching above it in a vase shape are 2-foot stems of Bowman's root (*Gillenia trifoliata*), a beauty from the woods of eastern North

Nowhere in the garden are variegated leaves as valuable as in shade, where their spots and stripes light up the shadows.

America whose shower of small white star-shaped flowers are accented by bright red calyxes. This graceful, early-summer bloomer, also known as Indian physic, and the look-alike species *G. stipulata* were once used in both Native American medicine and country healing.

American pennyroyal (*Hedeoma pulegioides*) is native to dry woods in eastern North America. It is valued for its sweet-scented foliage that looks a bit like basil and the tiny lavender flowers that bloom in summer. Large-flowered calamint (*Calamintha grandiflora*) makes a wonderful summer show in light shade with small rosy-lavender flowers that nearly obscure its mound of oval green leaves. Equally useful as an edging plant or to trail over rocks is lesser calamint (*C. nepeta*) with pink or white flowers and peppermint-scented foliage. The long blooming period and ease of culture make both calamints an indispensable part of our woodland plantings, especially to break up the monotony of broad-leaved hostas and pulmonarias.

LIGHT TOUCHES

Nowhere in the garden are variegated leaves as valuable as in shade, where their spots and stripes light up the shadows. It's no secret; clever gardeners have been employing variegated plants for a long time, but many more choice plants have recently been introduced. It might be possible to create an entire garden out of hostas, although the slug bait bills could prove prohibitive. Hybridizers have given the humble green-leaved hosta a host of extroverted personalities with an incredible array of stripes, edges, puckers, and all manner of variegation against fields of blue, gold, and every shade of green. Thumbing through the catalog of a hosta specialist is like inspecting a book of wallpaper patterns.

After a while, the eyes begin to blur. The current enthusiasm for hostas is reminiscent of the Victorian passion for fancy-leaved geraniums. While we doubt that all of the many hundreds of modern hosta varieties will survive the test of time, dozens of excellent variegated hybrids will continue to grace shady gardens and make good companions for shade-loving herbs.

Other shade-garden standbys get a crisp update as new variegated forms become more widely available. Two variegated forms of heartleaf (*Brunnera macrophylla*)—'Hadspen Cream' and 'Variegata'—have become very popular, but suppliers are hard-pressed to keep up with the demand because they grow slowly. The leaves' creamy margins stand out in subdued light even after the sprays of blue forget-me-not flowers have faded.

The ground-covering ability of bugleweed (*Ajuga reptans*) makes it a natural for enhancing shaded areas with clean-cut leaves and, in early summer, early blue bugle flowers. To add variety to the shade-garden tapestry, there are also bronze and deep green bugleweeds, as well as the variegated 'Burgundy Glow', with pink, maroon, and white markings, and 'Variegata', with white edges on its green leaves.

The white-rimmed leaves of honesty (*Lunaria annua*, also known as money plant) carry the show during the interval between flowering and the appearance of the flat, round, translucent seedpods. Don't be alarmed if seedlings initially fail to display the distinctive white edge. Rob gave away his first flat of variegated money plant, thinking that the seed company had mistakenly shipped the plain kind. Imagine his chagrin when the recipient called to rave about the impact of the flowers in concert

A woodland path weaves through three layers of growth: tree canopy, understory of azaleas and magnolias, and underplantings of variegated hosta, white comfrey, and blue brunnera.

with the variegated leaves. The white-flowered cultivar 'Alba Variegata' doesn't even bother to show its true colors until the second season, but it is worth the wait for the pairing of white flowers and white-margined leaves. (A friend who is no great fan of variegated foliage kidded us that our specimens appeared to exhibit symptoms of herbicide damage. It's refreshing to have

friends with varying—no, make that *variegated* tastes.)

Speckles and spots decorate the foliage of lungworts, which take their ungainly name from the erroneous medieval supposition that the shape of the leaves and their spots indicated that the plants could be used to treat chest complaints. Recent cultivars of *Pulmonaria* have been selected for

The enormous leaves of skunk cabbage rise from the mucky soil at a pond's edge, dwarfing Peltaphyllum peltatum *and chartreuse-flowering* Tellima grandiflora, *as well as bistort and hostas on the bank behind.*

DAVID RECALLS THE WOODS

Every year when I was growing up in the Midwest, my family indulged in the spring ritual of hunting mushrooms. It was a popular local sport; anyone who's ever enjoyed the woodsy taste of wild mushrooms knows why. As a child, I was always thrilled to spot a tawny gray morel peeking up through the leaves.

Weather permitting, we would stop in the woods on Sunday afternoons on our way back from visiting family and friends. One of my favorite spots was Grandpa Spittler's woods. My great-grandfather had owned this little patch of woodland along a creek, and he chopped trees here in the mid-1800s to build the house and barn where Grandpa Spittler was born. Another mushroom-hunting ground was Rocky Hollow, a stretch of woods along the edge of the prairie. We went there only in early spring when the rattlesnakes were still hibernating.

Just as we learned which mushrooms to pick and which to avoid, we came to know the early spring flowers that grew in the same areas—the mayapples, jack-in-the-pulpits, and spiderworts. We got scratched by the thorns of wild raspberries, blackberries, and greenbriar vines. Bleeding-hearts and Dutchman's-breeches were always enough to distract us from the mushroom hunting, as were the scarlet berries of bittersweet still on the vines from the previous year. The woodlands were decked with the white flowers of dogwoods and the rich purple of redbuds. When we came upon sassafras, we gathered young sprouts for tea. In addition to these treasures, there were box turtles to look for and birdsong to listen to.

Living now in the dry high plains of Colorado, near the pine-covered mountains, I miss the woodlands of the Midwest, especially in the spring. I try to get back during mushroom season as often as I can and make a trek through the woods. And in our Denver garden, I include some of the woodland plants that I grew up with, such as mayapples, trilliums, and spiderworts. I look forward to them as much as any other plants in the garden.

their spotting patterns; in some, such as 'Spilled Milk' or 'Excalibur', the spots have joined to become a bold splash of silver over most of the leaf. The spots are still apparent on the foliage of blue-flowered 'Roy Davidson', deep blue 'Benediction', or white 'Sissinghurst White'. The flowers are a lovely spring feature, but the season-long display of handsome foliage makes the lungworts invaluable to the shade gardener. The fact that slugs rarely eat the hairy leaves doesn't hurt either.

Prominent yellow spots decorate the rosettes of variegated London pride (*Saxifraga umbrosa* 'Variegata') and leopard plant (*Farfugium japonicum* 'Aureo-maculata').

Even the common columbine known as granny's bonnet (*Aquilegia vulgaris*) has been dressed up in a coat of gold-splashed leaves in new hybrids that usually pass their variegation on to their offspring.

WET AND WILD

The margins of a pond or meandering stream provide a perfect environment for plants that like to sink their roots deep into oozing mud. Marsh plants such as reeds, rushes, and cattails have supplied materials for building and weaving since the dawn of time. Our ancestors also gathered healing and culinary plants from the water's edge.

Cultivated for practical purposes by basketmakers, marsh reeds and grasses provide strong architectural elements for water features in the landscape. Variegated sweet flag (*Acorus calamus* 'Variegatus') grows several feet tall and its green blades are decorated with yellow stripes. Many species of rushes (*Juncus*) have ornamental foliage. We grow 'Carmen's Gray', which has narrow, dark olive-gray leaves. It is accented by the ever-fascinating horsetails (*Equisetum* sp.), or scouring rushes, once used as pot scrubbers before the invention of Brillo pads because of their high silica content. They're also used for strengthening hair and nails. (What gardener could not use extra-strong nails about the first of May?)

Pennyroyal (*Mentha pulegium*) thrives in moist shade on banks, as does the intensely fragrant Corsican mint (*M. requienii*). Also clinging to banks are lovely plants such as marsh marigold (*Caltha palustris*), with large lemon yellow flowers accenting its glossy green leaves. Cultivars such as 'Monstrosa', 'Multiplex', and 'Flore-Pleno' are treasured for their extra-large double flowers. Marsh woundwort (*Stachys palustris*) also grows in this habitat. Its slender stems and tiny pink flowers enhance the creamy white or pink sprays of meadowsweet (*Filipendula ulmaria*).

Houttuynia cordata comes from the Orient, where it is called *doku-dami*. The arrow-shaped leaves and especially the rhizomes are scented like a blend of orange and coriander and used in some traditional dishes. The cultivar 'Chameleon' has green, white, and deep pink leaves that make it an intriguing—if invasive—addition to damp areas. It may be best to confine it to a pot in a patio pond rather than unleashing it on the rest of the garden.

Bolder accents for a marshy spot include the water cannas, yellow flag (*Iris pseuda-corus*), and blue flags (*I. versicolor* and *I. missouriensis*). The grandest of them all is the unfortunately named skunk cabbage of western North America, *Lysichiton americanum*, with its glossy, bright green leaves and yellow-hooded flower spike in early spring. This native American receives scant attention in its homeland but is a big hit in Europe. Our friend Judy, who lives in New Jersey, remembers driving with Dutch gardening friends who insisted she screech to a halt whenever they spotted a stand of skunk cabbage along the highway.

MUCKING ABOUT

While a picturesque stream doesn't flow through every garden, many of us have some sort of wet spot. It might be a topographic feature of the land or the result of poor landscaping that funnels the runoff from an entire block into a gardener's backyard. Where the soil is clay, this soggy area can be a constant source of irritation and failed plantings. Changing the grade or installing drainage pipes can bust the budget. Investing instead in attractive bog-dwelling plants can turn a soggy site into a stunning showcase.

Shrubs and small trees that tolerate wet feet provide structure to the planting and a screen for property lines or unsightly features. The chokeberry (*Aronia arbutifolia* 'Brilliant') attracts birds with scarlet fruit followed by an impressive autumnal cascade of red leaves. Red-twigged tatarian dogwood (*Cornus alba*) and yellow-stem dogwood (*C. stolonifera* 'Flaviramea') create dense thickets that prove their worth in winter when the leaves have fallen to reveal the colorful bark. Pussy willow (*Salix caprea*) and dwarf arctic blue willow (*S. purpurea* 'Nana') also display their architecture best without a cloak of foliage but offer an interesting presence in summer as well.

River birch (*Betula nigra*), which thrives in mucky soil, is a handsome small tree with trailing catkins. Elder make good backdrops: accented by white flowers and dark fruit, the golden, cut-leaf, bronze, and variegated cultivars are especially effective.

> What gardener could not use extra-strong nails about the first of May?

Rheum palmatum makes an unforgettable impression high above a skirt of sweet cicely and forget-me-nots.

The transformation of the unsightly wet area continues with tall herbaceous perennials such as bee balm, button snakeroot (*Liatris pycnostachya*), swamp milkweed (*Asclepias incarnata*), queen-of-the-prairie (*Filipendula rubra*), joe-pye weed, New York ironweed (*Vernonia noveboracensis*), Culver's root (*Veronicastrum virginicum*), yellow coneflower (*Rudbeckia laciniata*), swamp mallow (*Malva palustris*), goldenrods, cardinal flower (*Lobelia cardinalis*), and great blue lobelia (*L. siphilitica*). That's quite a collection of surefire hits.

Somewhat shorter in stature, but equally gardenworthy, are snakeweed or bistort (*Polygonum bistorta*), with straight stems topped by oval heads of chalky pink flowers, and violet-blue-flowered vervain (*Verbena hastata*), both of which bloom in concert with daylilies and purple coneflower. All can put up with periodic flooding. While the linear foliage of moisture-loving Siberian iris (*Iris sibirica*), yellow flag, blue flag, and Louisiana iris contributes a strong vertical element throughout the season, the flowers dazzle in late spring and early summer.

SUBTROPICAL SURPRISES

Many of our herbal traditions— indeed, our horticultural practices at large—come from Europe. Whereas a great many plants from temperate climates have gained entry to Western horticultural circles over the centuries, plants from subtropical and tropical climates have remained outside. England became the repository of the great

Victorian plant hunters, but they often favored showy orchids or ferns likely to bring oohs and ahs from the crowds in the palm houses at Kew Gardens. The useful culinary and medicinal plants of the Tropics were not a priority, nor was northern Europe a suitable place to grow them.

Much of the United States is not the ideal habitat for many of these plants either, but the climates of the Deep South, West Coast, and extreme Southwest offer an opportunity to grow a wide range of herbs used by other cultures, even if we value them more for their ornamental qualities than for their usefulness. Bananas and elephant's ear, or taro (*Colocasia esculenta*), are two of the great workhorses of the Tropics, but home gardeners grow them primarily as novelties.

Tropical herbs with culinary or medicinal uses make intriguing additions to home gardens where they can be accommodated, even if they produce only a tiny crop or are not suitable for home remedies. We don't know too many Californians who rely on their caper bushes (*Capparis spinosa*) for a steady supply of the spicy little pickled flower heads, but the white flowers with their long white filaments are so interesting that it seems a shame not to grow them among the herbs and vegetables.

Herbs of Central and South America that make delightful garden accents include cannas, papaya, cashew, several palms, epazote, chile peppers, cacao, and several species of *Datura* and *Amaranthus*.

From Africa come castor bean, hyacinth bean, lion's ear (*Leonotis leonurus*), glory lily (*Gloriosa superba*), aloes, pelargoniums, and Madagascar periwinkle (*Catharanthus roseus*). Although usually grown for its pretty pink or white blossoms, the periwinkle's use in several cancer drugs has made it the echinacea of Madagascar.

Tropical Asia enriches our gardens with ginger, turmeric, bamboos, gotu kola (*Centella asiatica*), cardamom, pepper, nutmeg, cloves, mandrake, and sandalwood, as well as any number of herbs used in Asiatic healing that are only now becoming known to Western herbalists.

Many Australian plants perform well on the West Coast. The scent of eucalyptus on the breeze is today as much a part of California life as the sight of native golden poppies. Other herbal plants from Down Under that contribute to the horticultural scene include New Zealand flax (*Phormium tenax*), breadfruit (*Pandanus odoratissimus*), and several species of *Acacia* and *Prostanthera*.

Investing in attractive bog-dwelling plants can turn a soggy site into a stunning showcase.

The herbs and spices of the Middle East have long been incorporated into Western culture, so they don't come as much of a surprise when we encounter them in the garden. To us, they evoke images of ancient walled gardens where fountains splashed and ornamental gardening first flowered as an art. From humble dill, grapes, and onions to exotic frankincense, myrrh, and pomegranate, the plants of the Middle East are interwoven into history. Coriander, mustard, safflower, caraway, cumin, sesame, and alfalfa may not have the exotic cachet of a banana tree (or its dramatic impact), but they may be planted in small patches among more decorative plants to good effect. Specimens of olive, fig, myrtle, oleander, cedar-of-Lebanon, and many kinds of citrus can make a statement all on their own. Northerners who admire these handsome shrubs and trees can grow them, too, if they are willing to pot them and carry them to indoor safety every autumn. We're still waiting for the first crop from our tiny fig tree. Sure, we can pick up some nice figs at the supermarket, but where's the mystery of an Arabian night in that?

Chapter 5

THE DRYLAND GARDEN

I T TAKES ONLY an afternoon to fly from coast to coast. From a window seat on a New York-to-Los Angeles flight, one sees more than the grids of roads and checkerboards of fields. As the plane crosses the Great Plains, one sees the colors of the land change. Lush forests and fields give way to paler shades of green and tawny gold, and finally to muted tones of sage, gray, buff, and beige.

The western landscape, with its extraordinary geographic features, often bakes under a rainless sky. Its plant life, however, is supremely adapted to the mineral-rich but humus-poor soil, the dry air, summer heat, and winter cold. Transplanting an East Coast garden vision to the West takes water—a commodity whose increasing value limits the plants that can be grown well. Many stalwart herbs and ornamental perennials adapt beautifully, but others fail.

Western gardens are coming to include a broad palette of well-chosen plants. Once predominant greens are giving way to the colors of the native landscape—shimmering silver, dusty blue, sage green, russet brown, and sun-bleached yellow. These dryland herbs need not be planted in Death Valley Days fashion, with yards of gravel between each plant (and a wagon wheel or steer skull for accent). A garden that receives little or no supplemental irrigation can be a thing of beauty—full and lavishly planted, teeming with texture, color, scent, and variety.

Dryland gardeners have learned to incorporate compatible herbs that echo the beauty of the natural surroundings. Some are native while others originate in lands with similar climates, such as the Mediterranean region, Central Asia, the Middle East, and Eastern Europe. In the Southwest and along coastal California and Oregon, gardeners have taken great interest in the herbs and flowers of South Africa and the west coast of South America.

The need for water-wise plantings is not limited to the arid lands of the West. Within the past decade, many parts of the country have experienced prolonged droughts and water restrictions. It is estimated that 50 percent of a homeowner's water goes toward landscape maintenance.

The goal of water-wise planting doesn't have to be *no*-water plantings. All dryland plantings need to be watered the first year, but once they are established, many herbs will thrive on only 2 inches of water each month, and some require only half that much.

The soft, rounded shapes of stick-a-dove lavender and santolina echo the natural forms of the rocks in this California garden.

FIRST IMPRESSIONS: HELL STRIPS

One of the most difficult areas to maintain in any western garden is that narrow patch of lawn between the sidewalk and the street known in our part of the country as a hell strip. Trapped between a river of asphalt and a stream of concrete, the grass easily bakes to a crisp in hot weather. Drive

Prickles and spears abound in the hellstrip of plantsmen Sean Hogan and Parker Sanderson in Portland, Oregan. Plants include an unusual species of sea holly, Eryngium umbelliferum, *and desert spoon,* Desidilirion wheeleri, *backed by artemisia. Dogs with a mission avoid the area.*

garden that receives little or no supplemental irrigation can be
a thing of beauty—full and lavishly planted, teeming with
texture, color, scent, and variety.

through any western city in the summer and you'll see rivulets of water trickling down the gutters from at least one hell strip. There you'll find a sprinkler going, wasting water by overshooting the edge of the grass on both sides—not quite strong enough to offer a free car wash to motorists but more than enough to annoy passersby on the sidewalk. Truly desperate homeowners try, hose in hand, to bring the dead strip of grass back to life with a one-shot soaking. They probably won't live long enough to get it done. If any part of the home garden was meant for water-wise planting, this is it.

Some parts of the country normally receive sufficient rainfall to keep grass growing all summer long, even in the hell strips. Some years, however, none of us has grass that can make it through the August-September drought. Most grasses are accustomed to taking a prolonged summer vacation by going dormant during extended periods of drought and heat; only by keeping them on the life support of water and chemicals do they come through.

Dead and dying grass is an open invitation for opportunistic weeds. No matter how dry it gets for the lawn, it won't be too dry for the weeds. Knotweed (*Polygonum aviculare*) and goat's-head (*Tribulus terrestris*) are two that love the conditions that fry turf. Dandelions, bindweed, and lamb's-quarters aren't far from the mark either. As far as we're concerned, there's really only one solution: get rid of the turf.

The scorching summer sun may be inhospitable to bluegrass, but a wonderful array of herbs revel in the heat and drought. Any number of forms of *Dianthus* make a splendid show when they blossom in early summer. After we cut back the faded flowers, the

gray or green needlelike foliage is handsome until the snow flies. To edge the walk, we're especially fond of diminutive 'Tiny Rubies', whose bright pink flowers the size of a dime rise about 4 inches above a tight mat of gray-green leaves. Other pinks that thrive and self-seed in this harsh environment include cottage pink (*D. plumarius*) and maiden pink (*D. deltoides*).

Artemisia schmidtiana 'Silver Mound' performs admirably on this austere regimen and never opens up in the middle as it often does with more water and richer soil. Partridge feather, Greek yarrow, thymes, ice plant (*Delosperma* sp.), sunroses, dwarf bearded iris, tunic flower (*Petrorhagia saxifraga*), and Mount Atlas daisy (*Anacyclus pyrethrum* var. *depressus*) also stay compact and healthy. Self-sowing annuals take care of themselves. California poppies in pastel tones of pink and cream contrast with the vivid desert bluebell (*Phacelia campanularia*). It's an international mélange of plants, made possible precisely because the dry conditions approximate the plants' homeland conditions. Losses are minimal in winter, even for South African ice plants, because the roots don't rot in waterlogged soil.

City regulations often dictate that plants in the hell strip other than trees not exceed a foot in height, but we count on lax enforcement to enable us to leave the flower stalks of lamb's ears, snow daisy, and purple-blue Rocky Mountain penstemon (*Penstemon strictus*).

Our native prickly poppy (*Argemone platyceras*) is right at home in the unimproved, sun-baked hell strip in front of our house. Prickly poppy is sometimes called cowboy's fried eggs because its white petals encircle a yolk-yellow center. In several low-water areas of our garden, it appeared of its own accord, but it's a welcome addition. The glaucous foliage and tissue-paper-thin petals of the large, pure white blossoms elicit comments from even sophisticated gardeners. More than just a pretty face, prickly poppy has a long tradition in the West among native peoples as a healing plant.

The scorching summer sun may be inhospitable to bluegrass, but a wonderful array of herbs revel in the heat and drought.

Other western native herbs, such as blue prairie flax (*Linum perenne* subsp. *lewisii*), Indian blanket (*Gaillardia aristata*), hummingbird's trumpet (*Epilobium canum* subsp. *latifolium*), and Missouri evening primrose (*Oenothera macrocarpa*), also do well in the hell strip. In a low spot where runoff tends to collect, purple coneflower does fine.

Our neighbors seem delighted with the transformation of the long strip of formerly hideous lawn. Dogs ignore it, perhaps because they prefer green turf further down the street or perhaps because there are enough prickly plants like yucca and cactus to dissuade them from lingering. Children rarely pick the flowers, and we experience little vandalism, except for a larcenous collector who once dug up a rare species at night. We've learned to keep our choice plants in a fenced portion of the garden.

By replacing turf with herbs and flowers, we became pioneers in our own neighborhood, but the concept has been catching on from coast to coast. In some communities, there's already a strong tradition of pretty, drought-tolerant front gardens. A walk down almost any street in Berkeley, California, is a treat for an herb gardener. Silver mounds of santolina, lavender, and fleabane set off specimens of Mexican bush sage (*Salvia leucantha*), blue potato tree (*Solanum wrightii*), and pink naked ladies (*Amaryllis belladonna*). Orange and gold nasturtiums twine through clumps of blue agapanthus and calla lilies. Jasmine, wisteria, and bougainvillea hang from trellises and porches. Many plants appear to have been passed from neighbor to neighbor down the block. Gourds grow with caper bushes, amaranths with borage, and thymes with calendulas. There are few fences to protect these friendly front gardens, few signs pleading with pedestrians not to pick the flowers. In a locale where flowers seem to sprout from every patch of earth, there's little need to be possessive.

There are several things to keep in mind when planning a dryland planting in the hell strip. Don't underestimate the staying power of grass. It has an uncanny ability to go dormant in hot, dry weather and survive until growing conditions improve. If you want to convert that strip of lawn along the street into a flower bed, be sure that the grass is truly dead. There are many ways to kill a lawn, and we've tried most of them: chemical attacks, suffocation by plastic or newspapers, and cruel and premeditated neglect. The last is seldom effective.

Lemon mint, poppy, and cardoon make a handsome trio in our herb and vegetable garden.

The surest way to guarantee that the grass in the hell strip is dead is to strip off the sod and take it to the compost pile. This is the most labor-intensive method of turficide, but it's worth it in the long run. Not only is the grass gone, never to return, but stripping off the sod allows you to level the strip at or below the level of the curb to conserve natural rainfall. In most established neighborhoods, the hell strips build up over time so that they shed water, making hell-strip watering even less effective.

Second, till the soil. You need to overcome years of compaction. Grab a good shovel or spading fork and work the ground. This is the time to add any soil amendments that you want. In many places, you don't have too much to worry about. Many dryland plants are adapted to poor soils and resent too rich a mixture. Most

soils, whether sandy loam or heavy clay, need only a thin layer of compost. Dryland plants generally do fine in native soil conditions. A small amount of compost or other organic matter will lower the pH ever so slightly in an alkaline soil, and a light dusting of lime can sweeten an acid soil. The addition of organic matter loosens clay soil so that water can percolate downward, and it helps hold moisture in a sandy soil.

Organic matter also helps hold nutrients and make them available to plants.

Water-wise Borders

Many plants that originated in arid and semiarid regions have small, fine-textured, hairy or gray leaves that cut down on water loss, resist heat and wind, and reflect light rather than absorbing it. Although these

Away from the house, in the driest part of our pastel border, midsummer stars include
Verbascum bombyciferum *'Arctic Summer',* Agastache barberi, *gayfeather, sunflower,*
*Jupiter's distaff (*Salvia glutinosa*), and Russian sage.*

plants are visually interesting, a border made up solely of fine texture needs help, which comes in the form of bold plants with outstanding architectural qualities.

These high-impact herbs include sea kale (*Crambe maritima*), whose thick, waxy leaves look like lovely turquoise-blue cabbage. They unfurl quickly and dramatically in spring as stout stems more than a foot high produce clusters of creamy white blossoms. The inflated pods that follow are equally showy. The roots of sea kale can be dug and eaten, as Europeans have been doing for centuries. A visitor asked David if he dug the roots to eat. "Not at seven bucks a pop," he replied, referring to the going rate for a gallon-size plant at the nursery.

The smooth, slightly wavy leaves of horned poppy (*Glaucium flavum*) also have a turquoise sheen. They complement the crinkled, amber-yellow petals of the early summer flowers that are followed by long seedpods which grow and curve like the fingernails of an ancient Chinese concubine. This Mediterranean native has a tradition of herbal use in centuries past, now obsolete due to its toxic nature. The pods impart an unusual textural element to the garden or dried arrangements. Left to set seed, the plants usually behave as biennials or short-lived perennials.

The beautiful foliage rosettes of some mulleins are reason enough to grow them, but their flowering spikes make them indispensable in the dry border. *Verbascum bombyciferum* displays silver-gray leaves covered with a white cottony down that catches the sun with luminous highlights. The soft, sage-green leaves of miner's-candle (*V. thapsus*) also have a feltlike texture. *V. wiedemannianum* displays a rosette of olive green leaves in its first season.

Most mulleins are biennial, flowering in their second year. The flower stalks of *V. bombyciferum* shoot up to 5 feet or more. They are woolly white with lemon-yellow flowers, as are those of miner's-candle. The

common name refers to the practice of dipping the stalk in tallow and using it as a torch in western gold and silver mines. Patches of wild mullein still grow around many mountain mining towns, their towering spikes a reminder of the boom days. *V. wiedemannianum,* a recent introduction from Turkey, bears 3-foot spires of flowers in a luscious shade of grape purple set off by yellow stamens. This one is less productive than the other two, which self-seed prodigiously, and its seedlings need perfect drainage over the winter.

Mullein spikes are to the dryland gardener what delphiniums and monkshoods are

---

By replacing turf with herbs and flowers, we became pioneers in our own neighborhood.

---

to the gardener in a moist climate. They add both height and drama to the border. Most mulleins open their blossoms only in the morning; on sunny days they close by noon.

Many mulleins are highly ornamental, but not all are as drought tolerant as these three. Foliage color usually is a clue: those with lush green leaves, such as nettle-leaved mullein, *V. chaixii,* require more moisture. Its spikes grow about waist high or a bit more, thickly studded in early summer with yellow flowers with purple stamens. The form 'Album' has white flowers with a reddish-pink interior. A white form of moth mullein (*V. blattaria*), which is normally yellow, is even showier, with bigger, glistening white petals and plum-colored stamens.

Scotch thistle (*Onopordum acanthium*) is the king of architectural plants for the water-wise garden, or any other one for that matter. It's 6 to 8 feet tall (even taller with more moisture), and its spiny arms and purple thistle flowers scare the neighbors to pieces. Perhaps they fear a giant mutant strain of dreaded Russian thistle has invaded. Their concerns about a takeover in their yard are largely unjustified, as the seeds of this biennial plant are relatively heavy and fall close to the mother plant instead of floating on the breeze. We do take care to deadhead our Scotch thistle (except for a single flower head that ensures a handful of new plants) because it seeds like mad and could get out of hand.

The felty, scalloped leaves can grow to 2 feet or longer, and an entire plant may occupy a spot 5 feet in diameter. Leave room. There's a sharp spine between scallops on the leaves, and the stalk is also armed and dangerous—making it a bear to remove if you change your mind about its location at midseason.

The tiered spikes of Jerusalem sage (*Phlomis fruticosa*) are a splendid structural addition to dryland gardens. This shrub varies in height according to climate; it's cut down by a hard freeze but usually survives winter temperatures as low as 20°F. In frost-free areas, Jerusalem sage grows to 6 feet or taller with an equal spread, blooming from spring into summer with whorls of yellow tubular flowers. Its herbaceous perennial cousins include straw yellow *P. russeliana* and peculiar buff-and-olive *P. samia*—both hardy at least to Zone 5 and very drought tolerant—and three "pretty in pink" species, *P. alpina, P. tuberosa,* and *P. cashmeriana.* These pink-flowered species make desirable border plants, but none is noted for drought resistance, and *P. cashmeriana* actually prefers partial shade. Expect spikes 3 to 4 feet tall from all of these perennial *Phlomis,* whose characteristic stacked whorls stay ornamental even after the flowers fade.

BLOSSOMS IN THE DUST

The list of perennial herbs for a low-water border is a long and lovely one. For height and invigorating aroma, Russian sage (a *Perovskia atriplicifolia* hybrid) and agastaches make compelling focal points. The flowers of Russian sage are lavender. *Agastache barberi* covers its upright stems in bright, mauve-pink tubular flowers. The flowers of *A. cana* are bright pink, while those of *A. rupestris* are apricot. The fluffy lavender flower heads of anise hyssop (*A. foeniculum*) make pretty border accents and hold well into winter as they bleach to straw gold.

Lavender-blue meadow clary (*Salvia pratensis*) and clary sage (*S. sclarea*) get by with little supplemental moisture. Their flowers contribute to the full, lush look that belies the scant moisture a dryland border actually receives. Some gardeners prefer the deep blush of 'Turkestanica' clary, but the paler species has its charms. We've noticed that the future flower color is telegraphed by the coloration in the leaf stems of the young plants. A pink stem indicates vibrantly colored flowers. (The same trick works for detecting white-flowered foxgloves.)

Grecian foxglove (*Digitalis lanata*) takes to heat and drought the way *D. purpurea* takes to shade and water. Grecian foxglove has gray-green woolly leaves and a rigid stalk of whitish flowers with a delicate tracery of brown veins and a pale orange throat. Once established, it reseeds reliably. The upright 3-foot spikes of purple toadflax (*Linaria purpurea*) and the pale pink cultivar 'Canon J. Went' contribute a sprightly, delicate look that is appealing. The bold lavender-purple flower stalks of spike gayfeather (*Liatris spicata*) and western snakeroot (*L. punctata*) are the brightest exclamation marks of all in the dryland border.

The list of perennial herbs for a low-water border is a long and lovely one.

Predominantly fine-textured perennial herbs effortlessly endow the dryland garden with the billowing look that English border-makers strive so hard to achieve. It's easy to incorporate airy lavender German statice (*Goniolimon tataricum*) and willowy, long-blooming apple-blossom grass (*Gaura lindheimeri*). Artemisias, common oregano, and garden sage form graceful, flowing mounds that interlock perfectly with clumps of thyme, ballotas, marrubiums, pinks, and thrift. Spikes of many species of *Penstemon,* vivid orange butterfly weed (*Asclepias tuberosa*), and bearded iris rise from the rounded forms and draw all eyes in early or midsummer. Grown lean and mean, the iris are rarely bothered by borers or rot. The same regimen also prolongs the life of many perennials that would otherwise expire quickly after a few years of lush living.

Spreading, rambling herbs weave through the dry border. The round flower heads of prairie snowball (*Abronia fragrans*) exude a piercing sweetness in late afternoon. In early summer, rock soapwort (*Saponaria ocymoides*) smothers itself in vibrant pink flowers (a pretty white form has just been introduced), and kidney vetch (*Anthyllis vulneraria*) responds with clusters of bright yellow blossoms.

Bulbous herbs that tolerate periodic dry spells include white garlic chives (*Allium tuberosum*), blue garlic (*A. caeruleum*), chives, Turkish onion (*A. karataviense*), and garlic. On the West Coast, society garlic (*Tulbaghia violacea*) from South Africa thrives on neglect, forming large clumps of foot-tall grassy leaves topped by lavender-mauve blossoms. Saffron crocus (*Crocus sativus*) likes it really hot and dry. Planting this Middle Eastern native in a rich, moist soil is a death sentence.

Annuals for dryland gardening fall into the "no muss, no fuss" category. A bit of judicious thinning will keep their numbers manageable in the first few years of a new garden, but as the perennials expand, annuals must find a way to fit in, and they usually do. When introducing a new annual, we often loosen the soil surface in autumn, scatter the seed, and lightly tamp the soil. Many annuals sprout during winter and early spring. Once established, they retain at least a foothold. Besides the western gardener's best friend, California poppy, our annual favorites include golden yellow blazing star (*Mentzelia lindleyi*), night-blooming angel's-trumpet (*Datura innoxia*),

The threat of water restrictions pose no menace here: Mexican bush sage, santolina, Mexican fleabane, lavender, and bougainvillea have transformed a front lawn in Berkeley, California into a water-wise cottage garden.

borage, opium poppy, dill, larkspur, sunflower, bachelor's-button, and love-in-a-mist. To a lesser extent, summer savory, amaranths, safflower (*Carthamus tinctorius*), wallflower, dyer's coreopsis (*Coreopsis tinctoria*), and nasturtiums also cope well with limited irrigation. Rue, purple coneflower, catmints, hyssop (*Hyssopus officinalis*), wall germander (*Teucrium chamaedrys*), Jupiter's beard, and rose campion all do well in borders that ordinarily receive plentiful rainfall, but they can also endure periodic dry spells.

WONDERFUL WOODIES

Shrubs and small trees of the desert Southwest and Great Basin possess a

Armed and decorous, this agave withstands drought, salt sprays, and predators; to our eyes it's as beautiful as any rose.

strange, overpowering beauty forged by extremes of climate. For the indigenous peoples and Spanish colonists who lived in this hostile environment before the advent of air conditioning and highways, the native trees and shrubs were crucial to survival. They provided not only shade, but also fiber for weaving and basketry, wood for fuel, and juice, flesh, and flowers for healing and sustenance. Many of these plants have ornamental qualities and thrive with minimal care, demanding little of the coddling that shrubs imported from moister climates often do. Shrubs from dry, sunny climates perform admirably in the West.

In a dryland planting, these shrubs add height and substance and contrast with smaller herbaceous plants. Many offer varied textures, blossoms, seeds, pods, and bark for an extended season of interest. The finely dissected, dusty olive green leaves of fernbush (*Chamaebatiaria millefolium*), a 6-foot shrub similar to spirea, complement the summertime conical clusters of ivory flowers. Rabbitbrush (*Chrysothamnus nauseosus*), called chamisa in the Southwest, has been a source for dye, tea, and cough medicine. Butterflies and bees flock to its late-season display of golden yellow sprays accenting small gray leaves.

The powdered pods and leaves of several species of *Acacia* have treated a litany of complaints, from diaper rash and back pain to the sore flanks of horses. The drought resistance and fine-textured, brilliant yellow flowers of these small trees make them excellent subjects for a dryland garden.

Other useful shrubs include winterfat (*Ceratoides lanata*), a sagebrush look-alike with showy winter "wool" on silver leaves that are often grazed by livestock and wildlife; lead plant (*Amorpha canescens*), an elegant small shrub with panicles of purple flowers and gray-green leaves reminiscent of mimosa; and Siberian pea shrub (*Caragana arborescens*), a showstopper

The University of California at Berkeley Botanic Gardens takes on the appearance of an architectural exhibit with giants of the desert, including cactus and Agave americana. *These elaborate water storage structures are adapted to survive in some of the driest parts of the Southwest.*

in early summer with vivid yellow pealike flowers.

Cliff rose or quinine bush (*Cowania mexicana*) displays ¾-inch yellow roses on gnarled, architectural branches. A cliff-rose tea has been used for coughs and backaches. Many species and selections of manzanita (*Arctostaphylos* spp.) guarantee an extended period of garden interest with twisted branches, mahogany red bark, leathery olive green leaves, and pale pink, nodding flowers followed by red berries. The same may be said for Apache plume (*Fallugia paradoxa*), a member of the rose family whose ¾-inch pristine white blossoms are followed by flowery seed heads that look like beautiful feather

The dainty flowers of soapwort belie its tough-as-nails constitution, easily capable of surviving on natural rainfall long after the farmhouse it once grew around has disappeared.

dusters. When it's backlit by the setting sun, this shrub is an unforgettable sight.

Native Americans once used the young branches of skunkbush, or three-leaf sumac (*Rhus trilobata*), to weave baskets and the crushed fruits to make "lemonade". This small shrub, only 6 feet at maturity, is extremely useful for controlling erosion on steep banks and boasts good autumn foliage color. Prairie tribes made pemmican from buffalo meat, fat, and the purple berries of western serviceberry (*Amelanchier alnifolia*); the species has now been developed for commercial fruit production. White spring flowers and fiery autumn foliage add to the value of this small tree.

Many species of broom (*Cytisus*) thrive in dry soil; in fact, some species of this European import are outlawed in areas where they have naturalized too readily, so check before planting. Pealike, usually bright yellow blossoms cover a cat's-cradle maze of wiry stems. Mormon tea (*Ephedra nevadensis*) has a similar tangled structure with curious conelike yellow flowers followed by orange berries that look like jingle bells. This western native provided medicinal tea for settlers and may warrant research into its healing properties.

A small shrub of the Southwest, coyote mint (*Monardella odoratissima*), is difficult to overlook. Its powerful fragrance of peppermint is appealing, as are its lavender blossoms that resemble those of bee balm. Coyote mint grows about a foot tall and survives at least as far north as Denver but may succumb in wet clay soil. Texas bush sage (*Leucophyllum frutescens*), sometimes called Texas ranger, now ranges outside its home state as gardeners in New Mexico, Arizona, and Southern California have discovered its attractive form, gray foliage, small blue flowers, and ease of culture.

The silhouettes of brooms and ephedras make an important contribution to the garden in winter, as do the overused junipers. Many a house has disappeared behind an impenetrable mass of junipers initially planted to disguise a concrete foundation;

some junipers are even made to suffer the indignity of being sheared into poodle cuts. Junipers don't have to be ugly; many are downright handsome. Get them away from the house and into the border, and select varieties that stay relatively compact. There are dozens to choose from, including such stellar performers as *Juniperus squamata* 'Blue Star', 3 feet tall and aptly named for its steely blue foliage, and *J. horizontalis* 'Prince of Wales', only 4 to 6 inches tall with blue-tinged, bright green foliage—both turn

---

Annuals for dryland gardening fall into the "no muss, no fuss" category. A bit of judicious thinning will keep their numbers manageable.

---

shades of lavender in winter—and *J. horizontalis* 'Blue Chip', less than a foot tall with prostrate blue-green foliage.

Among upright forms of juniper, *J. chinensis* 'Robusta Green' boasts an informal, irregular growth habit reminiscent of an Italian cypress. Looking as if it were sculpted by wind and snow, it fits well into a naturalistic planting; it may reach about 15 feet tall. 'Gray Gleam', 'Moonglow', and 'Wichita Blue' deserve consideration as backdrop specimens, their gray foliage setting off the flowers and foliage of low-water herbs. All are pyramidal and may reach 20 feet after several decades.

Single pink, delightfully fragrant blossoms make the native western wild rose, *Rosa woodsii*, a perfect partner for junipers. The plant puts up with the worst in soil and weather, but allow room for its suckering roots. With TLC, the rose will form a dense thicket fit to encircle Sleeping Beauty's castle. Romance surrounds the yellow rose of Texas (*Rosa × harisonii*), which traveled West with early settlers and put down roots. They are deep ones that enable it to cope with tough conditions which turn lesser roses into instant potpourri. The double yellow flowers appear reliably in late spring or early summer—perhaps with musical accompaniment from proud Texans, wherever they live.

POINTS OF INTEREST

In the Southwest and along the West Coast, aloes, agaves, and yuccas make bold statements. They survive the worst of droughts, storing moisture in their thick leaves. Some are equipped with sharp barbs to deter desert animals that might otherwise feast on them. *Aloe vera* from the Canary Islands is well known to herb gardeners for its use in soothing burns, but a number of other *Aloe* species have similar uses as well as unusual, decorative structures. Native Americans used agaves for fiber and fermented the juice. Among the most sensational of the clan is the century plant (*Agave americana*), reputed (incorrectly) to bloom only after a hundred years. It grows into a whopping specimen over time, with enormous glaucous gray spines, finally sending up a flowering spike so tall (20 feet or more) that some have been known to break through the glass roof of a greenhouse. Variegated cultivars are even more impressive—if that's possible—with a crisp, cream-colored stripe running down the center of each leaf. Where cold winters make it impossible to leave agaves and aloes in the ground, they can be moved indoors for easy care in pots.

Hardiness is rarely an issue in growing yuccas. Southeastern Adam's-needle (*Yucca filamentosa*) and western soapweed (*Y. glauca*) are glorious marvels at any time of the year. The flowering stalks display white flowers with crepe-textured petals. The rough brown pods, with burnished gold interiors, punctuate the autumn and winter landscape.

Other spiny plants with sculptural qualities and showy blossoms include prickly pears (*Opuntia* sp.), whose juice and flesh have been used much like that of *Aloe vera* to relieve burns and bruises, while a tea brewed from the flowers has traditionally been used to treat diabetes. To treat coughs and inflammations, the Apache made a tea from the tubular scarlet flowers of ocotillo (*Fouquieria splendens*), though it would seem a perilous job to pluck them from the top of the ocotillo's viciously spined stems.

MEDITERRANEAN INFLUENCE

Among Mediterranean shrubs, West Coast gardeners have long used lavenders, santolinas, curry plant (*Helichrysum italicum*), and rosemary (*Rosmarinus officinalis*). Northerners envy these gardeners for their ability to grow rosemaries, with their haze of blue or occasionally white or pink flowers cloaking the strongly structured branches. The hardiest of the lot is 'Arp', an open, upright cultivar with lavender flowers and lemon-scented gray-green leaves. Named for the Texas town where it was found, 'Arp' is hardy to −10°F, making it suitable for Zone 6 or warmer.

Other upright rosemaries include three pink-flowered varieties, 'Pinkie', 'Majorca Pink', and 'Roseus', the white 'Albus' and the dark blue 'Tuscan Blue', pale blue 'Miss Jessop's Upright', and free-flowering 'Sissinghurst Blue'. Prostrate types that spill over walls or tumble down slopes include violet-blue 'Severn Sea', dark blue 'Fota Blue', and sky-blue 'McConnell's Blue'. All of these cultivars also demonstrate differences in their growth habits and the color, shape, and taste of their leaves.

Bay (*Laurus nobilis*) makes a strong presence in many West Coast gardens; clipped topiary specimens can emphasize formality where appropriate. California bay (*Umbellularia californica*) has attractive clusters of yellow flowers in spring and leaves that resemble those of culinary bay. When crushed, they release aromatic oils that smell like a cross between witch hazel and camphor; they should not be used in cooking. The tree, which may reach 80 feet in height, is also called California laurel or headache tree for its herbal properties.

Chapter 6

EVERY NOOK AND CRANNY

G ARDEN PATHS AND dry-stacked walls can harbor tiny plants that would otherwise be lost in the rest of the garden. We like to fill our paths and walls with lovely little things that are a pleasure to grow, touch, and sniff. The ground-hugging and wall-climbing herbs, alpines, perennials, and annuals invite us to linger, to lean in for a closer look.

While we're grateful someone invented cement to hold house bricks together, we "mortar" the spaces in our walls and paths with a wide variety of small herbs and other decorative and useful plants. Many plants, especially those of Mediterranean origin, welcome the opportunity to spill onto the warm, dry stones as their roots delve into the crevices between, conditions that mimic those of their native habitats. A wall built without mortar offers similar cracks from which the plants can cascade down the stone surface.

Plants for filling nooks and crannies need to be tough but not overly aggressive. Size is a matter of preference. Gardeners with classic rock-garden sensibilities favor tiny, compact alpine plants. We know a few rock gardeners who pull up any plant that dares to expand an inch beyond its allotted space. It's understandable why they make these rules, though: tiny buns and tuffets are likely to be buried under an overly aggressive neighbor. Our jumbled perennial borders are hardly the place for small plants, either. Even at the edges of the beds, the small ones are in constant danger of being smothered by a rambunctious cranesbill, lady's mantle, or lamb's ears. At our place, the cracks and crevices of the pathways belong to the little fellas.

Our first path project fifteen years ago was fairly simple. After sledge-hammering and removing a crumbling concrete walk, we laid a straight path of bricks. About every 2 feet, we left an 8-inch gap and planted it with bird's-eye veronica (*V. filiformis*). The result was pretty, especially in late spring and early summer when the azure flowers appeared, and the only maintenance that we had to do was occasionally peel off mats of veronica that encroached too far onto the brick. One summer in our vegetable garden, we installed a similar path, substituting various low-growing thymes and oreganos for the veronica.

Lamb's ears and Laurentia fluviatilis *soften the angular lines of a flagstone walk in a California garden.*

Tightly laid brick or cobblestone paths offer little growing space, so it's necessary either to leave gaps in the pattern or create an edge with room for planting. Stone paths, especially those of randomly spaced flags, offer the greatest possibilities for pockets. Where flagstones are available, it is relatively easy (depending on your strength and stamina) to make a run to a supplier, select and load pieces, take them home, and

lay them. Our soil is naturally sandy, so we merely rake an area smooth, then lay the flagstones jigsaw-puzzle style. It takes a little fiddling, wriggling them back and forth and raking extra sand underneath to level each piece, but the flags remain fairly stable. If your soil is heavy clay, dig it out to a depth of 6 inches before laying the stone and fill the depression with a mixture of one-third soil, one-third compost, and one-third washed coarse sand. This mix will provide a suitable medium for growing a wide variety of plants.

In selecting plants, consider how much traffic the path will bear. Plants living in a walkway to the front door will get stepped on more frequently than those in a more secluded part of the garden. Also consider the amount of water that falls on a pathway, its exposure to sun, and the site's drainage.

UNDERFOOT

The champion plants for a sunny garden walk are the thymes (*Thymus*). The tightest, lowest-growing forms are most useful for a heavily trafficked path. Some of the best of this group are cultivars of *T. praecox* subsp. *arcticus.* (The taxonomy of this genus has been undergoing revision, and you'll find the various forms listed under a wide variety of botanical Latin names.) Red-flowered thyme ('Coccineus'), woolly thyme ('Lanuginosus'), and pink creeping thyme ('Elfin') are all just 1 to 3 inches tall. 'Minus' is the smallest of the genus, making compact, slow-growing blue-green clumps of minute leaves with equally diminutive lavender flowers. All can take a moderate amount of foot traffic. Taller forms, such as lemon thyme (*T. × citriodorus*) and common thyme (*T. vulgaris*) and its cultivars, are best planted at

Our front garden has little structure except for flagstone working paths softened by sedums and thyme, and nearly hidden in early summer by veronicas, mallows, and rose campion.

the edge of a path rather than directly between stones.

A word of caution. Bees love thyme flowers, wherever they grow. If someone in the family is allergic to bee-stings, choose other plants. Barefoot gardeners may want to stick to woolly thyme and 'Minus', which flower rarely or lightly.

For a wide path such as the one to our potting shed, where it's sunny and the soil stays fairly moist, strawberries fill in quickly. The reddish tone of the flags sets off the pink flowers of 'Pink Panda', which are followed by small but tasty berries. This lovely strawberry needs no coddling. One plant is all you'll ever need to buy because 'Pink Panda' makes many runners, great for filling a large area fast but otherwise invasive. We mix in thyme and pussy-toes (*Antennaria rosea*) with the strawberries for variety. The thyme's fine leaves contrast with the larger ones of the strawberry, while pussy-toes forms mats of silver foliage topped in early summer by pink-tinted cat's-paw flowers. A dwarf species, *A. parvifolia*, is more compact and suitable for cracks as small as an inch wide.

Along the edges of the path to the potting shed, where there is little chance of their getting trampled, we grow sweet Williams and other dianthuses, dwarf irises, coral bells, nodding onion (*Allium cernuum*), and sea pinks (*Armeria maritima*), including the dwarf selection 'Victor Reiter'. Salad burnet also sprawls onto this path, but we are very careful to deadhead it before it seeds by the millions into the cracks.

The narrow flagstone paths that thread through the front-yard garden are designed for access to the plants and are just wide enough for one gardener and a bushel basket, or perhaps a friend. We had to block them off during a recent summer's

Plants for filling nooks and crannies need to be tough but not overly aggressive.

he champion plants for a sunny garden walk are the thymes.
The tightest, lowest-growing forms are most useful for a heavily trafficked path.

garden tour sponsored by the local public television station, fearing that 600 pairs of feet would devastate the plants growing in the cracks. Thyme can take a little traffic "in stride" but not the equivalent of a Busby Berkeley chorus line.

Because we designed the front-yard garden to thrive on minimal supplemental moisture, the plants that fill the cracks in these narrow paths or spill out across them are not only small but drought resistant. They include the cobweb houseleek (*Sempervivum arachnoideum*), which looks like a spider has spun a delicate white web inside each of its small rosettes; pussy-toes; and creeping Spanish cinquefoil (*Potentilla nevadensis*), a pretty 4-inch-tall ground cover with sage green leaves and simple, five-petaled yellow flowers. Double bird's-foot trefoil (*Lotus corniculatus* 'Pleniflorus') hugs the ground tightly, its tiny blue-green leaves topped by minute pealike golden flowers. The trefoil creeps between stones, rarely venturing onto the hot surface.

The low mats of filigreed green leaves of Mount Atlas daisy (*Anacyclus pyrethrum* var. *depressus*) are topped in April and May with showy blossoms, each white ray exposing a maroon-red underside when it closes for the evening. Other small daisies bloom alongside the path beside low-growing annuals such as sweet alyssum, love-in-a-mist, and portulaca. A number of low-growing sedums soften the lines of path stones. These include gold moss sedum (*Sedum acre*) with yellow flowers over 2-inch-tall mats of minute, fleshy evergreen leaves; *S. kamtschaticum*, with yellow stars over a 4-inch-tall sprawling mat of toothed leaves; and *S. spurium* 'Dragon's Blood' with deep pink blossoms topping sprawling red foliage. Prostrate veronicas contribute mats just a few inches tall and flower in shades of blue

or pink. These varieties include Turkish veronica (*Veronica liwanensis*) with deep blue flowers in May, *V. oltensis* with a shiny mat of leaves and lighter blue blossoms, and woolly veronica (*V. pectinata*) with pink or blue flowers in spring.

Herb gardeners who like the common yarrow (*Achillea millefolium*) may not be familiar with shorter species that grow only 6 to 8 inches tall and are drought tolerant. Greek yarrow (*A. ageratifolia*) bears creamy flowers over finely cut green leaves. Serbian yarrow (*A. serbica*) blooms with pure white flower heads above gray leaves, and woolly yarrow (*A. tomentosa*) also has white flowers that complement its hairy mats of leaves.

Mountain sandwort (*Arenaria montana*) forms 3-inch-tall mounds of beautiful large white flowers, while Spanish sandwort (*A. tetraquetra*) is an inch shorter. Sandworts bloom in early summer and do best, as you may guess from their names, in sandy, well-drained soil.

Two species of catchfly are also suitable for pathway plantings. In early summer double white campion (*Silene alpestris* 'Flore Pleno') forms a loose, 2-inch tall mound of green leaves and a spray of white flowers similar to baby's breath. Fall catchfly (*S. schafta*) saves its pretty pink flowers until late summer, appearing on 6-inch stems. They're ideal counterparts to the frothy white profusion of tunic flowers (*Petrorhagia saxifraga*), just a few inches taller and spreading as wide as a dinner plate.

Ground-hugging Corsican mint (*Mentha requienii*), with its refreshing scent, is great for paths in very moist places. English daisies can also be allowed to self-sow in cracks where moisture is regular. In moist spots in mild climates, baby's tears (*Soleirolia soleirolii*) can be used to soften the lines of paths or trail around stepping stones.

*The flagstones of this Denver patio seem to float like pieces of ice in a sea of lady's mantle,
thymes, and ice plant, finally breaking on a shore of pink evening primrose, yarrow, and daylilies.*

Cascades of thyme tumbling down an old set of steps soften the stonework and lend an air of even greater antiquity. Gardeners who regularly entertain herds of teenagers would find their thyme-covered steps trampled to mush.

Golden feverfew, columbines, and Irish moss turn a wall of recycled concrete into an inviting seating area in this West Coast garden.

DOWN THE PRIMROSE PATH

Few images in gardening are as evocative as the words "primrose path". Perhaps some of us have been led down one figuratively, but few of us have a real one on our property. The opportunity to build one exists, however, in a partially shaded area with sufficient moisture. The idea of a pastiche of colorful plants beneath our feet is reminiscent of *The Unicorn in Captivity,* the haunting, fifteenth-century French tapestry of a fenced unicorn in a field of flowers now hanging in the Cloisters in New York City. In our woodland garden, the path materials vary, but we favor old brick or stone. Where the path creeps beneath an old apple tree near the irrigation ditch, we've covered it with a layer of pine needles. They crunch beneath our sneakers as we meander by.

Along these shady walks, we've planted the old reliable primroses of England, cowslip (*Primula veris*) and oxlip (*P. elatior*). With their modest yellow bells, they're not as showy as the modern hybrids, but neither do they attract every slug in the county nor die off every winter. At their feet, in a mod-ern interpretation of a medieval look, we've tucked in woolly thyme, which tolerates more shade than one would expect, and double Roman chamomile (*Chamaemelum nobile* 'Flore Pleno'), which releases a delightful fruity fragrance when trod upon. Emerald green Irish moss (*Sagina subulata*) blooms with tiny white stars early in the season and fills in between paving stones or on the edge of the path. *Mazus reptans,* a trailer with small leaves and lavender or white flowers that look like small snapdragons, also fills in tight spaces. The colorful leaves of carpet bugle (*Ajuga reptans*) provide contrast, as does 'Atropurpurea' with bronze leaves and 'Burgundy Glow' with variegated leaves in shades of pink, purple, and white. Both cultivars bear short spikes of small blue flowers in early summer over the 3- to 6-inch-tall clumps of leaves. Further foliage variation is provided by variegated strawberry, which suffers terribly in hot sun; golden moneywort (*Lysimachia nummularia* 'Aurea'), with prostrate golden green leaves and yellow flowers in early summer; and small ivies with cream margins that accent their deep green leaves.

*A rocky slope suits Lebanese oregano, with its showy chartreuse bracts and tiny flowers vividly
underscoring house leeks and the unfurling trumpets of gentian.*

ROB: THE SIMPLE SEMPS

My friend Panayoti Kelaidis, rock alpine curator at the Denver Botanic Gardens and a renowned plantsman, gave me some unusual hens-and-chicks (*Sempervivum*) years ago. I still recall his telling me, "Some of the greatest horticulturists started their careers growing semps." Perhaps this was his way of reminding me to appreciate even the humblest of plants. He did not know that when I was in the second grade, my sister and I built our first rock garden in the backyard and planted it with creeping phlox, sedums, and hens-and-chicks.

Our neighbor Katie, my first gardening mentor, had teased the little chicks gently from the patch that grew behind her house. Hens-and-chicks grow so quickly and easily that I'm sure she figured they would give confidence to a budding gardener. They did, but then I moved on to grow many other wonderful plants and forgot all about them for a long time.

The genus *Sempervivum* excites dedicated collectors, but few herb gardeners pay attention to it. Europeans of old would plant hens-and-chicks on roofs to keep lightning from striking the house. The plants require little moisture and will seemingly thrive in a thimbleful of the poorest soil. Better yet, the juice of the succulent leaves is an old-fashioned treatment for bee and wasp stings, which you might get crawling around on the roof repairing broken tiles.

Nowadays, our Denver roof is about the only place we *don't* grow some sort of *Sempervivum*. The tiniest ones live in our alpine troughs. The bigger ones survive in containers that accent parts of the garden. They spill from old enamelware pots grouped near the potting shed. They fill wide, shallow clay pots perched on brick columns at the ends of the backyard borders. They even colonize an old wine barrel on the back patio. Hens-and-chicks look their very best clumped along stone paths and basking between rocks.

Dead nettles (*Lamium maculatum*), despite their unfortunate name, have handsome leaves splashed with metallic silver that provide beauty throughout much of the year. The plants are gorgeous in spring when they bloom: the names 'White Nancy' and 'Shell Pink' aptly describe their flowers, while 'Beacon Silver' is deep pink. Dead nettles sprawl too much to be suitable between cracks, but at 3 to 5 inches they stay low enough for inclusion alongside paths, where we can easily trim them if they get out of hand.

Self heals (*Prunella grandiflora* and *P. laciniata*) are similar in growth and appearance, with dark green foliage and pink or purple blossoms. Two dwarf lady's mantles, *Alchemilla glaucescens* and *A. alpina*, provide a bright spot of chartreuse just inches above soil level and add to the Old World charm we're after.

Clumps of Labrador violet (*Viola labradorica*), with bronze leaves and purple flowers, and long-blooming rose-purple Corsican pansy (*V. corsica*) provide punctuation points along a path. The tight leafy masses of cockleshell bellflower or fairies' thimbles (*Campanula cochleariifolia*) are enlivened in mid- to late summer by lavender bells dangling just 2 inches off the ground. Johnny-jump-ups (*Viola tricolor*) and edging lobelia (*Lobelia erinus*), usually grown as annuals, fill a similar role.

Small bulbs are a delight blooming between stones and along paths in partial shade. Crocuses, snowdrops, striped squill

(*Puschkinia scilloides*), Siberian squill (*Scilla siberica*), and chionodoxa gladden a gardener's heart in early spring. Baby cyclamen (*Cyclamen hederifolium*) and autumn crocus (*Crocus spectosus*) close the growing season with flowers that belie the calendar with springlike freshness. They push through ground-cover plants with seemingly little effort and disappear relatively unobtrusively. We leave the foliage to mature before removing it.

WALLS AND ROCKY SLOPES

We don't have a proper rock garden, but we have built a retaining wall from lichen-covered native stone on the west side of the house. We lugged stone for several days for this project, which let us level a modest slope so that we could lay a brick dining patio. The wall is about 40 feet long but only 2 feet tall. When we picture what hell must be like, we imagine hauling rock for a stone wall that never ends.

If you're building a wall on a sloping site, keep a few things in mind. Set the rocks at an angle with the tops sloping back into the bank. This will help keep the soil in place and create planting pockets. Rather than putting down rocks in one uninterrupted plane, stack a row of rocks to several feet high, then fill in behind it with soil. Raise a new tier to that level, perhaps 8 inches back toward the slope, and fill in behind it, and so on. By carving steps out of a slope, you create more space for planting. If your existing soil is acceptable, use it for backfill. Otherwise, mix in compost or fresh topsoil to create a soil suitable to the plants you wish to grow.

There are bound to be trouble spots wherever two rocks meet and the soil does not stay in place. Plug these immediately with hens-and-chicks, the superglue of the plant world.

> Small bulbs are a delight blooming between stones and along paths in partial shade.

In our wall, we left plenty of room between stones and filled it with fast-draining sandy loam. We've planted it with whatever strikes our fancy, although we keep in mind that a stone crevice suits some plants and not others. Some plants seem at home in the flowering wall, others are out of place. Prim bedding plants look downright silly, but a wide range of other plants, particularly those with an informal look and a tendency to sprawl, combine well. At the shadiest end, we grow small ferns, forget-me-nots, self heal, dead nettles, and dwarf columbines.

In the sunniest parts, we've got a strange assortment of perennial ornamentals and herbs, including small campanulas, bergenia, St.-John's-wort, calamint, and hedge woundwort (*Stachys sylvatica*), with 3-foot-tall spikes of white-spotted, claret red flowers and leaves that were once widely used as poultices for swollen lymph nodes. We're content to simply enjoy its modest floral display.

In the smallest cracks sprout thick clusters of hens-and-chicks, drabas, rock cress, and sedums. Springtime brings a flush of Siberian squills, miniature narcissi, and species tulips. As the wall disappears under the spreading branches of an old Engelmann spruce, the white flowers of sweet woodruff, and mock strawberry (*Duchesnea indica*) with yellow flowers followed by red fruit, take over as ground covers.

It takes time for plants to fill in a path or wall. As they do, a garden takes on an air of maturity and harmony. By selecting the right plants for specific conditions, a gardener extends the palette of plants to include the little charmers that might otherwise be overlooked. In softening the lines of these hardscape elements, they offer pleasant scents, pretty flowers, and striking foliage. Fill your own nooks and crannies, and you may find yourself lingering a few moments longer on garden strolls.

Chapter 7

THE POTTED HERB

A COLLECTION OF POTTED herbs is great when space is tight, but even when it's not, containers open avenues for growing tender and exotic herbs that might otherwise be impossible in cold-winter regions. Growing herbs in containers is a wonderful way to bring the outdoors to your doorstep. Even if you have the same herb growing in the border or herb garden, it's often more convenient to pinch a leaf from a patio pot that's just a few steps from the kitchen.

Although many people keep pots of herbs on the kitchen windowsill, they sometimes don't get beyond a bedraggled specimen of basil and an annual or two. But it's possible to grow as many striking combinations in containers as in beds and borders, and the same basic elements of garden design apply. Different herbs may be displayed in a single pot or in separate pots that are grouped together. The first option requires forethought, while the latter is often a matter of whim.

A collection of a favorite kind of plant, such as scented geraniums, may be effectively displayed in a cluster of similar, simple pots to emphasize the individual characteristics of each variety, or they can be scattered about to provide a note of continuity. Displaying container plants on a patio or deck is an art in itself. The same ideas about contrasting foliage and harmonious color combinations apply, but container size, height, and shape are also important.

As a general rule, fairly large containers offer the best chance for success outdoors. Except for cacti, succulents, and a few other very heat- and drought-tolerant plants, or unless you're clever enough to engineer a drip irrigation system or feel inclined to water more than once a day in very hot weather, plants need outdoor containers that are at least 14 inches in diameter. There is no maximum size; if you can muster the brute force to handle very large containers, they're fun to try, but keep in mind the work they will entail being moved about.

Another advantage of growing herbs in pots is that plants with different soil and water requirements can sit side by side—succulents next to heliotrope, for example—which is not possible in the garden. On the other hand, daydreaming is a liability when one has the hose in hand, and it takes a lot of concentration to skip over the dittany of Crete, aloes, and agaves while giving the mints, castor beans, and passionflower a thorough soaking.

Visitors are sometimes astonished at the diversity of our container plants. South African ice plants sit next to Mexican kalanchoes and agaves. Mediterranean bay and oleander meet Australian eucalyptus and

Following our axiom of "foliage first", the varied forms of scented geranium, the exotic foliage of voodoo lily, and the striking bronze leaves of perilla make a visually exciting display without flowers.

Asian ginger. A pot of New Zealand flax flourishes beside Malaysian voodoo lily (*Sauromatum venosum*). The fragrant, white-edged leaves of a form of Cuban oregano (*Plectranthus amboinicus*) tumble from a pot flanked by a ferny Mexican jacaranda, a variegated Oriental bamboo, and Oriental lilies. Strange bedfellows, indeed, but none are here simply because they're strange. Some familiar herbs, such as lemon verbena and chocolate mint, are clustered by the door for convenience, but most earn a place for their beauty. Fragrance—from night-blooming jasmine, nicotiana, lilies, scented geraniums, and heliotrope—is a wonderful addition to any patio.

The culinary herbs that we grow the most of are basils (*Ocimum* spp.). Like the mints and scented geraniums, basil now comes in many scents and flavors and leaf colors. Rounded, compact 'Spicy Globe' and 'Piccolo Verde' are perfect for pots, looking almost like clipped domes of tiny boxwood. 'Aussie Sweetie' is another good choice because its late-flowering stems need less pinching than other varieties. 'African Blue' has fragrant, dark green foliage with a blue cast and showy lavender flowers. 'Red Rubin' has spicy deep bronze leaves while the similar 'Purple Ruffles' has crinkled foliage and a mild taste. A green version with crinkled leaves is attractive and tasty (but the name 'Fluffy Ruffles' leaves us cold). Adventurous cooks should seek out 'Anise', 'Cinnamon', and 'Thai Lemon' basils, all with unusual flavors. Anise basil is our favorite in salads and usually elicits rave reviews from guests. We also like 'Mrs. Burns' Lemon', a strong-growing southern favorite.

Classic Italian basils include richly flavored 'Napoletano' with luxuriant light green leaves and 'Genova Profumatissima'

Simple but smart: a box topiary floats above a pool of golden creeping oregano in Rosemary Verey's English garden, proving, once again, that stunning containers need not be all blossom.

*Herbs can be as prim and proper as you please: a classic terra-cotta container
displays a centerpiece of rosemary and heliotrope while a pot of lemon grass achors
one corner of the barberry and box knot.*

with dark green leaves that carry an exotic scent almost like perfume. Both varieties are excellent for making Italian pesto or French pistou.

Mints come in many more flavors than spearmint and peppermint. You can enhance your tea with leaves of orange mint, apple mint, pineapple mint, lavender mint, and chocolate mint, to name just a few possibilities. Six leaves of chocolate mint placed in the filter before brewing make a

pot of coffee that will knock your socks off. Many mints grow too aggressively to be allowed in the garden, so pots are a good way to curb their wandering ways.

GETTING POTTED

Because cold or rainy winters can spell doom for many Mediterranean or tropical herbs, the obvious solution is to grow them in pots that you summer outside. Although almost anything can and probably has been used as a container, unglazed terra-cotta is the most sensible choice for a number of reasons. Wood, partially glazed pottery, and hypertufa (a mixture of peat, perlite, fiberglass, and cement) offer many of the advantages of terra-cotta and are generally far superior to plastic containers.

Even during rainy weather, these pots drain quickly. The biggest advantage of clay pots is that they are porous enough to allow both water and air to pass through. A clay pot absorbs water from the potting mix, and evaporation from the entire surface of the pot keeps the plant's roots from cooking in the summer sun. Anyone who has ever dumped out a gallon plastic nursery container that's been sitting in the sun will realize how hot the roots can get in these little solar cookers. At nurseries, container plants are grouped together in growing areas to shade the plastic from the scorching rays of the sun, but this isn't always easy to accomplish in a deck or patio setting. A terra-cotta pot provides the plants with conditions much closer to those in the ground.

Plant roots, no less than plant leaves, require air for growth. Even bog and water plants have special adaptations to either trap air among the roots or supply the roots with oxygen by some other means. When plants die from overwatering, it's really death by drowning. They don't get enough oxygen to function and they suffocate.

Soak terra-cotta pots before you use them. This is a annual ritual that we sometimes skip with older containers but always attend to with new clay pots, which are so porous and thirsty that they will absorb tremendous amounts of water. A clay pot that hasn't been properly saturated with water provides so much chance for evaporation that it's nearly impossible to keep the

Growing herbs in containers is a wonderful way to bring the outdoors to your doorstep.

soil inside moist. In such cases, the best thing to do is completely submerge the pot in water. We keep a large plastic trash container filled with water by the side of the house. When we bring home new clay pots (which it seems we're always doing), we unload them from the car directly into the waiting barrel. The air escaping will form tiny trails of bubbles much like a glass of champagne. When the bubbles stop, the pots are thoroughly soaked. Whether planted later the same day or sometime in the next week, they're always well soaked before we fill them with potting mix.

Potting mixes for containers should be light and freely draining. Soilless mixes composed of a large proportion of peat or compost stay waterlogged for a long time and turn to peat bricks when they dry out—neither of which is good for growing plants. A good potting mix should contain a fairly high percentage of material such as coarse sand, perlite (a volcanic glass that's been roasted and popped like popcorn), or vermiculite (an expanded mica) to make it drain well. You can make your own potting mix from these ingredients, but a general-purpose potting mix is fine for most herbs.

Don't be tempted to use soil from your garden in containers; it doesn't drain well, and it's almost always a serious mistake. Because potting mix is expensive, especially when you buy it by the bag, recycling it can be a major cost-saver.

We grow nearly 500 containers of plants each year but keep only a fraction through the winter. In late fall, we store the mints and any other potted hardy perennials that we want to save in a shady place mulched with leaves or straw to insulate them from excessive freezing and thawing, which can damage both pot and plant. Pots of tender perennials such as bay, lemongrass, rosemary, scented geraniums, Spanish and French lavender, and Cuban oregano live on our sunporch during freezing weather.

The threat of the first frost is always a call for action in the garden. At the first prediction of freezing temperatures, we begin seriously editing our potted plants: the banana

Too tender for winter in the open, potted rosemary standards are displayed amid box hedges during the summer in a Pennsylvania garden.

has to go inside this instant, but that scraggly abutilon can freeze; the bush basil won't survive even a light frost, but the cactus can live through temperatures in the upper teens. Gardeners in warm-weather regions probably can't appreciate how useful a hard freeze can be for honing down a collector's gone-mad taste in tender plants.

All the pots with plants that we haven't chosen to overwinter need to be emptied before the really bad weather sets in. We unceremoniously dump them into garbage cans—potting mix, foliage, roots, and all— to wait for the next spring. (The trash cans need to have drain holes to prevent the soil in the bottom from becoming waterlogged and sour.) Some of the larger plant parts can be relegated to the compost pile for future chipping or shredding, but most plants will decompose in the cans over winter, helping to enrich the old potting mix. By spring, we have garbage cans full of potting mix that we sieve through a screen and mix with a generous amount of fresh compost—whereupon it's ready for the next season of container gardening. This storing and mixing of potting mix generally ensures that any less-than-perfect batches get mixed into the rest and don't cause problems the second year.

We store our empty pots outside over the winter. Denver is blessed with dry winters, and although we lose a few pots each year,

most survive under the eaves of the house, away from the drip line. In wetter areas, it's a good idea to keep clay pots inside where they won't crack from repeatedly freezing and thawing. As the weather begins to warm up in spring, we begin staging the pots on the patio, deciding where the plants that have been stashed indoors will go. After the danger of the last frost is past, we fill the pots to prepare for spring planting.

LOCATION, LOCATION, LOCATION

The next step is the planting. A primary consideration, as in designing beds and borders, is choosing the right plants for the location (and vice versa).

Almost any deck, patio, or high-rise balcony can support a wide selection of herbs. Most culinary herbs require at least half a day of sun to develop good flavor. Many can take the full brunt of the sun on a patio that faces west or south as long as they are kept thoroughly watered. Others need some protection, and still others thrive in shade. Culinary herbs can be grown by themselves or combined with complementary ornamentals, as long as you use no pesticide harsher than soap. We apply either a balanced general-formula fertilizer every two weeks throughout the summer or a slow-release type that lasts most of the summer. Whenever plant performance stalls, as it often does in midsummer when roots compete for nutrients in a pot, we give everything a blast of fertilizer high in potassium.

The cascading leaves of licorice plant provide a perfect foil for a pink heirloom geranium, lobelia, 'African Blue' basil, sweet-tasting Aztec herb (Lippia dulcis), and the variegated foliage of Cuban oregano and Japanese hops vine.

Perennial herbs may be planted in outdoor pots after a few days of hardening off, gradually exposing them to more direct sun each day. Hardy herbs such as oreganos, artemisias, savories, chives, sages, and thymes thrive in the bright sun. Suitable annual companions include basils, scented geraniums, dill, fennel, nasturtiums, and gomphrenas. Perennials that tolerate partial shade include most mints, ginger, myrtle,

Potted herbs and ferns lend an air of intimate, relaxed charm in this New Orleans courtyard.

golden oregano, and other gold-leaved herbs. Plants treated as annuals that perform in partial shade include parsley, licorice plant, and species of *Plectranthus*.

GORGEOUS GROUPINGS

An assortment of potted herbs and ornamentals can add appeal to a windowless wall or highlight an unusual architectural feature such as an arch or alcove. Pots can emphasize an easily overlooked entrance or set of steps or distinguish a lackluster porch or landing. Many city gardeners have learned the hard way that front-porch pots should weigh several tons, be bolted down or glued, and contain some poison ivy so at least we have the satisfaction of knowing that the pot-nappers herniated something or at the very least developed a rash.

A single giant pot or half-barrel can make a statement in any setting—if its contents grow up, and out, and down. Spikes and vase-shaped plants provide the height and vertical lines, mounds and sprawlers fill in the middle ground, and trailers give that all-important, jam-packed, there's-a-green-thumb-in-the-family statement. A big

A grouping of perilla, Salvia coccinea, S. viridis, *marigolds, and verbena anchor the base of this Victorian arbor in Lucy Hardiman's Portland garden. They also hide the rose's spindly legs.*

pot needs something big in it, but monstrous is even better. A half-barrel of marigolds can become visually compelling when a whopping banana, canna, bay tree, dwarf fruit tree, or palm has been plopped in the middle. Marigold roots never get to the bottom of the barrel anyway, so there's plenty of room down there for roots that delve deeply.

We love rolled-rim Italian clay pots. We have dozens of them in many sizes, some with garland swag motifs or scallops or other whimsies of the potters. This classic shape usually calls for a planting with height. We often set a large rolled-rim pot on a block of wood or cinder block to lift it up even farther, then cluster smaller pots near its base to repeat the theme and disguise the staging.

Where we want to do a bronze, silver, and pink theme near the edge of our goldfish pond on the patio, we put our very best rolled-rim on a steady support of cinder blocks. In it, we stuff giant purple fountain grass (*Pennisetum alopecuroides* 'Burgundy Giant'), a dwarf red-leaf barberry, a single rose called Carefree Wonder, and fuzzy-leaved geraniums with the scent of peppermint. Other large pots that cluster around this central pot contain a bright pink oleander, several gray-leaved *Plectranthus argentatus*, and pink Asiatic lilies.

At their feet, we place shorter tubs with a navy glaze. (Unless a pot contains a long-term resident like the oleander, it's easier on the back to move these pots around while they're empty.) We've found that the blue glaze enhances many shades of flower and foliage. While sorely tempted to buy pots glazed in hunter green, jade, sand, and yellow ochre, we've had to draw the line somewhere. In the navy pots we keep a shocking pink mandevilla, pink penstemons, and a huge silver cloud of *Artemisia arborescens,* a graceful Mediterranean shrub that we doubt would prove hardy in the ground here. These we complement with small pots of succulents.

Pots of Artemisia *'Lambrook Silver', palms, and purple princess flower* (Tiboucina) *line the garden walks at Wave Hill in New York.*

In other spots on this pool patio, or the dining patio, or in shade beneath the folly, we use the same display ideas, setting the most attractive pots on sturdy supports and hiding the construction with more mundane terra-cotta containers. We also make use of benches and tables to hold prize specimens and our prettiest pots—anything to get them up. We've learned this from the placement of products at the supermarket: if you want something to be noticed, put it at eye level.

An island of containers can break up a long stretch of patio or terrace: use the biggest and tallest in the center and work outward going down. On a balcony or deck, pots of plants can hide a bad view or form a windbreak of dense, wind-resistant shrubs such as junipers.

This kind of staging brings variety to outdoor living areas. There's little reason to put up with a boring patio, porch, or deck. The ingredients for a private oasis are pots, soil, and imagination. Forget conventional dictates about "appropriate" patio plants. Grow what your heart tells you to. Our hearts tell us to experiment with all the green stuff we can get our hands on. Some might view our potted jungles and ask why. We simply reply why not?

ROB'S WATER DANCE

Some people are daunted by the prospect of tending as many potted plants as we do. I suppose that we are extreme, but gardeners need to get into the routine of watering patio pots whether they have five or five hundred. During the hottest, driest period of high summer, that means every day.

It takes me about twenty minutes. I twist a spray attachment onto the hose and let 'er rip. The water guzzlers get a deep, long drink, while the desert and Mediterranean plants get only a splash; cacti usually get ignored altogether. It has become second nature to me now to work my way around and give each plant the amount of water it requires.

The watering routine is necessary but not very stimulating. That's why I often put on my headphones and hook a tape player to my belt while I water or perform other sorts of repetitive gardening chores. I need energy, so I prefer loud, soaring music. Whether it's Mahler or Madonna, the chores fly by when I've got a headful of music. My problem, which has embarrassed me several times, is that I'm not content to merely listen to music: I've got to move. Maybe I'm related to Carmen Miranda.

One hot, dusty afternoon I was performing a primitive rumba as I snaked the hose across the patio when I noticed our neighbor Kathleen, who often drops by for a stroll in the garden. She's a lovely person and, incidentally, a nun; she no longer dresses in the old-fashioned habit, so I suppose she's a plain-clothes nun. I waved at her, then noticed about fifty people with her. They had come to see the garden, not the strange dancing gardener.

Kathleen says our garden is blessed. I don't know about that, but maybe it doesn't hurt to have a nun in the neighborhood. I do feel that the work we put into the garden rewards us many times over. For every disappointment, there are a hundred triumphs, but who's keeping score? The pleasure is in the process. People who don't garden may never quite understand why we do what we do, but perhaps they find satisfaction and joy in another kind of endeavor. I hope they do. That, indeed, is being blessed.

The contrasting shapes and textures of variegated fuchsia, marguerite daisy, licorice plant, impatiens, and variegated ligularia transform a simple rolled-rim pot into a work of art.

FAVORITE HERBS FOR INTERMINGLING

This reference chart provides descriptions of the herbs discussed in the text. Wherever possible we have based these descriptions on our own experience gardening in the Rocky Mountain West. We're fallible. Sun and soil are fallible. Plants are sometimes fallible, sometimes tough as nails. Please take these variables into account when using this information. ❧

Name	Hardiness Zones	Height/Spread	Flower Color/ Season of Bloom	Notes
ACHILLEA. Yarrow, milfoil. Compositae. Perennial herbs mostly native to Europe and Asia. Drought tolerant. Rock gardens or paths; borders, wild gardens or meadows. A. millefolium is the main species used herbally but only one of many useful in the garden.				
A. 'ANTHEA'	4–9	18–24 in./ 18–30 in.	pale yellow/ summer	Pretty with lavender and bellflowers.
A. 'MOONSHINE'	3–9	24 in./18 in.	sulfur yellow/ summer	A summer showstopper, effective with variegated iris.
A. AGERATIFOLIA Greek yarrow	5–9	6–10 in./ 6–10 in.	white/summer	A good choice for hell strips or rock gardens with alkaline soil.
A. FILIPENDULINA	3–9	4 ft./3 ft.	golden yellow/ summer	Showy plants that shouldn't be penalized because of their popularity; cultivars include 'Coronation Gold', 'Gold Plate', 'Parker's Variety'.
A. MILLEFOLIUM YARROW	3–8	2 ft./ indefinite	many colors/ summer	Aggressive but useful in dryland gardens; cultivars include pink-red 'Cerise Queen', red 'Fire King', orange-red 'Paprika', dark red 'Red Beauty', 'White Beauty', 'Lavender Lady'.
A. PTARMICA SNEEZEWORT	4–9	2 ft./indefinite	white/early to midsummer	Invasive but useful when paired with other thugs; selections include double-flowered 'Perry's White' and 'The Pearl', and shorter, somewhat less invasive 'Snowball'.
A. SERBICA SERBIAN YARROW	4–8	6 in./12 in.	white/May–June	Gray foliage makes a good show all summer in hell strips.
A. TOMENTOSA WOOLLY MILFOIL	4–8	6 in./12 in. or more	yellow/ summer	Gray-green foliage; excels in rock gardens for dry soil and full sun but performs poorly in hot and humid climates.
ACONITUM. Monkshood, wolfsbane. Ranunculaceae. Perennial herbs, most with tuberous roots, native to northern temperate regions. Full sun or partial shade; moist soil. Many garden species. A deadly poison, wolfsbane has been remarkably effective in keeping wolves out of our garden.				
A. NAPELLUS GARDEN MONKSHOOD WOLFSBANE	4–8	4–7 ft./ 1–3 ft.	indigo-blue/ mid- to late summer	Impressive, deep-toned spires for vertical accents; 'Album' has white flowers.
ACORUS. Sweet flag. Araceae. Perennial herbs native to Asia and North America grown for their ornamental foliage. Bogs to shallow standing water.				
A. CALAMUS SWEET FLAG	4–9	3 ft./ 1–3 ft.	greenish/ summer	A structural pond or streamside plant with mid-green sword-shaped leaves. 'Variegatus' has green and white striped leaves, often flushed with pink in spring.
A. GRAMINEUS JAPANESE SWEET FLAG	6–9	1 ft./ 1–2 ft.	insignificant/ summer	Evergreen with dark green linear leaves; 'Pusillus' is only about 10 in. tall; 'Variegatus' has creamy white striped leaves.
ADIANTUM. Maidenhair fern. Pteridaceae. Cosmopolitan genus of dainty terrestrial ferns. Full shade; moist, well-drained, humus-rich soil.				
A. CAPILLLUS-VENERIS	9–10	6–14 in./ 12 in.	none	Arching fronds, and lobed, fan-shaped leaves contrast with those of pulmonarias.
A. PEDATUM MAIDENHAIR FERN	3–8	18 in./ 18 in.	none	A sensational foliage plant for woodlands with emerald, finely-divided leaves.

Name	Hardiness Zones	Height/Spread	Flower Color/ Season of Bloom	Notes
AGASTACHE. Giant hyssop. Lamiaceae. Aromatic short-lived perennials native to North America, China, and Japan. Full sun to partial shade; well-drained ordinary soil.				
A. CANA	5–9	3–4 ft./ 1–3 ft.	pink/summer	This native of Arizona and Mexico puts on a fine show with minimal irrigation; wonderful fruity fragrance.
A. *FOENICULUM* ANISE HYSSOP	5–9	3–5 ft./ 1½–2½ ft.	lavender blue/ summer	Though it seeds too freely for our taste, the fluffy, anise-scented flowers make it worthwhile; 'Alabaster' has white flowers.
A. *RUPESTRIS*	5–9	3–5 ft./ 1½–2½ ft.	apricot/ late summer	The unusual flower color invites innovative pairing with bronze foliage.
AGAVE. Century plant. Agavaceae. Long-lived succulent herbs native to North and northern South America; plants of many species die after flowering once. Tolerant of drought, salt spray. Architectural plants for dry or wild gardens and sunny herbaceous borders; container plants in colder regions.				
A. *AMERICANA*	8–10	15–20 ft./ at least 4 ft.	greenish yellow/ winter or spring	This native of southwest North America and Mexico blooms when 15 to 50 years old, then dies; flowers fragrant. 'Marginata' has yellow leaf edges; 'Medio picta', with yellow-striped green leaves, is even more dramatic.
ALCHEMILLAE. Lady's mantle. Rosaceae. Hardy perennial herbs native to northern temperate regions and high-altitude Tropics. Sun to partial shade.				
A. *ALPINA*, ALPINE LADY'S MANTLE	3–7	4–8 in./ 4–8 in.	chartreuse/ summer	A small charmer with palmate, toothed leaves for edging paths or rock gardens.
A. *VULGARIS*	4–9	2½ ft./ 2½ ft.	chartreuse/ summer	The quintessential cottage garden plant that looks great with nearly everything except plastic flamingos.
ALLIUM. Onion. Liliaceae. Biennial or perennial bulbous or rhizomatous herbs native to the Northern Hemisphere and Africa. Bulbs have varying water requirements but most need sun.				
A. *CAERULEUM* BLUE GARLIC	4–9	30 in./8 in.	blue/June and July	True blue flowers look great waving above small catmints or pinks.
A. *CEPA* ONION	4–10	36 in./ 6–12 in.	white/ late spring	Biennial: flowers in second year then dies. The flowers are amazingly attractive.
A. *CERNUUM* NODDING ONION	4–9	12–18 in./ 12 in.	pink to purplish red/ June and July	Almost too pretty to be an onion; pendant flowers are delightful with sweet Williams and bellflowers.
A. *CHRISTOPHII* STARS-OF-PERSIA	5–9	12–18 in./ 8 in.	metallic lavender/ summer	Despite rumors to the contrary, performs better in partial shade in moderately moist soil; enjoy the 4–8 inch dry flower heads.
A. *FISTULOSUM* WELSH ONION	4–10	12 in./ 6–9 in.	yellow-white/ summer	The most widely cultivated allium in the Orient; pair with thyme or marjoram.
A. *KARATAVIENSE* TURKISH ONION	5–9	10 in./ 10 in.	grayish white/ May and June	Hot, sunny, dry spots suit this onion in our Denver garden. Broad leaves and large umbels are dramatic growing through Mt. Atlas daisy.
A. *SATIVUM* GARLIC	4–10	12–36 in./ 9–12 in.	green-white to pink/summer	Don't miss the loop-de-loop of the flowering stems; deadhead to keep little garlics from popping up through dunesilver planted at its feet.

Name	Hardiness Zones	Height/Spread	Flower Color/ Season of Bloom	Notes
A. SCHOENOPRASUM CHIVES	3–10	12 in./ 12–18 in.	mauve /late spring–early summer	Employ its linear foliage to accent lady's mantle or yarrows.
A. TUBEROSUM GARLIC CHIVES	3–9	20 in./ 20 in.	white/late summer	Combine the sweet-scented flowers with the gray foliage of pinks and artemisias.

ALOE. *Liliaceae. Succulent perennial herbs, shrubs, or trees native to Africa, Arabia, and the Cape Verde Islands. Full sun; well-drained soil. Container plants in colder regions.*

A. VERA ALOE	8–10	2–3 ft./ indefinite	yellow/summer	Make use of its thick, toothed leaves as a bold container specimen.

ANETHUM. *Dill. Umbelliferae. Aromatic annual or biennial old-world herbs. Full sun.*

A. GRAVEOLENS	Annual	24–48 in./ 12–15 in.	chartreuse-yellow/summer	Finely dissected, glaucous foliage adds an airy look to borders. It's too pretty only to be used for pickles.

ANGELICA. *Angelica. Umbelliferae. Biennial or short-lived perennial herbs native to the Northern Hemisphere. Full sun or dappled shade; moist, fertile soil.*

A. ARCHANGELICA	4–9	6 ft./3 ft.	white/summer	The bright green leaves and showy flower heads make angelica a focal point in cottage gardens or borders.

ARTEMISIA. *Sagebrush, wormwood, mugwort. Compositae. Mostly aromatic annual, biennial, or perennial herbs or shrubs native to northern temperate regions, western South America, and South Africa. Full sun; most tolerate drought and poor soil. Flowers inconspicuous.*

A. × 'HUNTINGTON'	5–10	2½ ft./ 2½ ft.	yellow/summer	The silver foliage serves as a foil for broad-leaved plants.
A. × 'LAMBROOK SILVER'	5–10	2½ ft./ 2½ ft.	yellow/summer	Finely cut silver leaves are especially effective in low light.
A. × 'POWIS CASTLE'	6–10	2–3 ft./4 ft.	yellow/summer	Fine-textured clouds of silver foliage set off white-flowered iris or lavatera to perfection.
A. ABROTANUM SOUTHERNWOOD	5–10	3 ft./1–2 ft.	yellow/summer	Var. *limoneum* is known as tangerine southernwood; it not only smells good but has a soft, pleasing texture.
A. ARBORESCENS TREE WORMWOOD	7–10	3½ ft./ 3½ ft.	yellow/summer	Strongly aromatic silver foliage.
A. CALIFORNICA CALIFORNIA SAGEBRUSH	8–10	2 ft./2 ft.	yellow/summer	Compact selections include 'Canyon Grey' and 'Montana'.
A. CANESCENS	5–9	10 in./24 in.	yellow/summer	Its reindeer-moss texture is very pleasing contrasted with sea hollies or horehounds.
A. FRIGIDA FRINGED SAGE	3–9	1 ft./2 ft.	yellow/summer	Gleaming foliage, particularly showy at dusk or dawn.
A. LUDOVICIANA PRAIRIE SAGE	3–9	2–4 ft./ indefinite	yellow/summer	Selections include 'Silver King', 'Silver Queen' and 'Valerie Finnis'; none is well behaved but all are worth confining.
A. PONTICA ROMAN WORMWOOD	5–10	15 in./ 12–24 in.	yellow/summer	A runner that may be allowed to weave its finely cut, gray-green leaves among equally rambunctious perennials.
A. PYCNOCEPHALA SANDHILL SAGE	5–10	24 in./ 18 in.	yellow/summer	Compact, extra-silver 'David's Choice' is said to be hardy to Zone 5.

Name	Hardiness Zones	Height/Spread	Flower Color/ Season of Bloom	Notes
A. STELLERIANA DUNESILVER, BEECH WORMWOOD	3–9	6–15 in./ indefinite	yellow/summer	Nearly white felty leaves; 'Silver Brocade' is more prostrate.
A. VULGARIS MUGWORT	4–10	2–5½ ft/ 1–3 ft.	yellow/summer	Red-purple stem, dark green leaves with silvery undersides. Variegated form available.
ATRIPLEX. *Orach, saltbush. Chenopodiaceae. Cosmopolitan annual herbs and shrubs. Full sun or partial shade (especially golden orach); any soil; many species tolerate salty or alkaline soil.*				
A. HORTENSIS ORACH	Annual	24–48 in./ 6–12 in.	inconspicuous/ summer	Gold ('Aureus') or burgundy ('Rubra') leaves; showy seed heads. Deadhead to prevent reseeding (both come true from seed).
BORAGO. *Borage. Boraginaceae. Hairy annual or perennial herbs native to the Mediterranean region. Used by the Romans to drive away melancholy,* B. officinalis *can brighten a sunny border.*				
B. OFFICINALIS	Annual	12–36 in./ 8–20 in.	blue/summer	'Alba' has white flowers and hairy foliage. Plants may have variegated foliage.
CALAMINTHA. *Calamint. Lamiaceae. Aromatic perennial herbs native to Europe and Asia. Most suited to dry sunny borders or containers.*				
C. GRANDIFLORA BEAUTIFUL MINT	5–10	18–36 in./ 24 in.	pink/June to August	Lovely mound of flowers to spill over a wall or at the front of borders. 'Variegata' has cream-streaked foliage.
C. NEPETA LESSER CATMINT	5–10	8–30 in./ 24–36 in.	pale violet to white/summer	Peppermint-scented leaves; C. *n* subsp. *nepeta* has more flowers and larger leaves.
CALENDULA. *Marigold. Compositae. Annual or perennial herbs native to the Mediterranean region. Sun to partial shade; moderately moist soil.*				
C. OFFICINALIS CALENDULA, POT MARIGOLD	Annual	8–20 in./ 6–12 in.	yellow to orange/spring to autumn	Although calendula poops out in the heat, self-sown plants make a good early display with bulbs.
CROCUS. *Crocus. Iridaceae. Cormous herbs native to the Mediterranean region.* C. sativus *is the only species used herbally (as both dye and seasoning). Full sun; dry soil.*				
C. SATIVUS SAFFRON CROCUS	4–9	6 in./6 in.	lilac-purple/ autumn	Sterile form that has apparently always depended on humans for propagation; the red stigmas are saffron, the world's most expensive foodstuff.
CYNARA. *Compositae. Thistlelike perennial herbs native to the Mediterranean region and Canary Islands. Sun to partial shade; moderately moist soil.*				
C. CARDUNCULUS CARDOON	7–10	3–6 ft./ 2–4 ft.	purple/summer	Frequently grown as an annual in cooler regions for its large architectural foliage but has occasionally wintered over in protected spots of our Zone 5 garden.
C. SCOLYMUS ARTICHOKE	7–10	3–6 ft./ 2–4 ft.	purple/summer	'Northern Star' is recommended for shorter growing seasons.
DIANTHUS. *Pink, carnation, sweet William. Caryophyllaceae. Annual, biennial, or perennial herbs native to Eurasia and the mountains of Africa.*				
D. × *ALLWOODII* ALLWOOD HYBRIDS	4–9	10 in./ 12 in.	white, pink, rose, salmon, purple, or bicolors/ summer	Time-honored selections include dark-eyed pale pink 'Daphne', semidouble pink 'Essex Witch', and salmon pink 'Helen'.

Name	Hardiness Zones	Height/Spread	Flower Color/ Season of Bloom	Notes
D. BARBATUS SWEET WILLIAM	4–9	6–18 in./ 8–12 in.	red, white, or pink/summer	Short-lived perennial often grown as an annual or biennial. No cottage garden is complete without them.
D. CHINENSIS CHINESE PINK	4–9	6–12 in./ 6–12 in.	white, pink, red, or multicolored/ summer	Often grown as an annual but better in its second season and sometimes beyond; numerous cultivars; good in alkaline soils.
D. DELTOIDES MAIDEN PINK	4–9	8 in./18 in.	pink, white, or cerise/summer	Small but numerous brilliant flowers; drought tolerant once established.
D. GRATIANOPOLITANUS CHEDDAR PINK	4–9	6–15 in./ 12–20 in.	bright pink/ summer	'Tiny Rubies' has bright pink double flowers on 4-inch stems. It's a particular favorite at the edge of our hell strip.
D. KNAPPII	5–9	24 in./ 8–15 in.	yellow/ midsummer	Only species with yellow flowers, borne on graceful, slender stems.
D. PLUMARIUS cottage pink	4–9	12–18 in./ 18 in.	white or pink/ June to July	Gray foliage is attractive year round, but the early summer flowering is glorious.

DIGITALIS. *Foxglove. Scrophulariaceae. Biennial or perennial herbs native to Europe, northwestern Africa, and central Asia.*

D. LANATA GRECIAN FOXGLOVE	4–10	36 in./ 10–15 in.	cream with orange and brown markings/ summer	Biennial or short-lived perennial, but self-sowing; ours thrive on drought and neglect.
D. PURPUREA COMMON FOXGLOVE	4–10	24–48 in./ 10–20 in.	purple, pink white, or apricot/ summer	Since they reseed poorly in drier climates, we sow seedlings in flats in June and plant them out in early autumn.

ECHINACEA. *Purple coneflower. Compositae. Hairy perennial herbs native to eastern North America. Large daisies have drooping ray flowers and prominent, cone-shaped central disc. Sun or partial shade. Tolerate drought, humidity.*

E. PURPUREA PURPLE CONEFLOWER	3–10	48 in./ 18–24 in.	purple/summer	'White Swan', with white flowers, grows to about 18 inches tall.

EQUISETUM. *Horsetail, scouring rush. Equisetaceae. Spore-bearing rushlike perennial herbs found worldwide except in Australia and New Zealand. Sun to partial shade; damp soil. Can be pernicious weeds.*

E. ARVENSE FIELD HORSETAIL	6–10	8–32 in./ indefinite	no flower	Almost as much sculpture as plant. Thin jointed stems can be pulled apart like pop beads.
E. HYEMALE COMMON SCOURING RUSH	3–11	28–36 in./ indefinite	no flower	For that primeval touch. Unusual accent with cannas, coleus, and all things tropical.

EUPATORIUM. *Boneset, Thoroughwort, Compositae. Perennial herbs and scrubs native to the eastern United States and Eurasia. Sun or partial shade; moist but well-drained soil.*

E. CAPILLIFOLIUM DOG FENNEL	6–9	9 ft./4 ft.	ivory/late summer and autumn	A wild beauty of the southeast finally becoming valued for its shaggy-dog foliage and impressive stature.
E. PURPUREUM JOE-PYE WEED	3–10	4–10 ft./ 2–6 ft.	pink/late summer	'Bartered Bride' is white; 'Gateway' is a shorter selection. We like the great big ones and so do the butterflies.

Name	Hardiness Zones	Height/Spread	Flower Color/ Season of Bloom	Notes
FOENICULUM. *Fennel. Umbelliferae. Aromatic biennial or perennial herb native to Mediterranean Europe. Sun; well-drained soil.*				
F. VULGARE FENNEL	4–10	4–8 ft./ 1½–4 ft.	sulfur yellow/ summer	'Purpureum', bronze fennel, makes a smoky haze that serves as a splendid backdrop for poppies, irises, and almost everything else.
GALIUM. *Bedstraw, cleavers. Rubiaceae. Annual or perennial herbs native to temperate regions.*				
G. ODORATUM SWEET WOODRUFF	3–9	12 in./ indefinite	white/early summer	A takeover artist that can be put to good use beneath shrubs where little else will survive; wood hyacinths pop through its white flowers effectively.
G. VERUM LADY'S BEDSTRAW	3–9	2–3 ft/ 1½–3 ft.	yellow, with lime cast/ early summer	A good long show of flowers and seed heads, but stalks may need support to prevent flopping.
GERANIUM. *Cranesbill. Geraniaceae. Annual or perennial herbs and subshrubs native to temperate regions. Sun or partial shade; moist but well-drained soil.*				
G. MACULATUM WILD GERANIUM	3–8	30 in./ 18 in.	pink/ summer	'Albiflorum' has white flowers; 'Chatto' is lavender pink; we love it with epimediums and wood hyacinth.
G. PLATYPETALUM	3–8	3 ft./3 ft.	purple/ summer	A perfect companion for peonies; mature plants grow as big as a bushel basket.
G. ROBERTIANUM HERB ROBERT	3–10	12 in./ 20 in.	deep pink/early summer to late autumn	Very small flowers; a charming colonizer or self-sowing nuisance, depending on your point of view.
HAMAMELIS. *Witch hazel. Hamamelidaceae. Deciduous shrubs or small trees native to North America, Europe, and eastern Asia. Sun or dappled shade; moist but well-drained soil.*				
H. VIRGINIANA	4–9	15 ft./10 ft.	yellow/fall	Pretty pale flowers when little else is blooming.
HEDERA. *Ivy. Araliaceae. Evergreen woody vines native to Europe, Asia, and northern North Africa. Partial to full shade; rich moist soil.*				
H. COLCHICA PERSIAN IVY	5–10	climber to 50 ft.	none	'Goldheart' has variegated foliage that is valuable in shade.
H. HELIX ENGLISH IVY	4–10	climber to 50 ft.	none	Roughly 300 named varieties, some only hardy to Zone 6.
HELIANTHUS. *Sunflower. Compositae. Showy annual or perennial herbs native to North and South America. Full sun; ordinary garden soil.*				
H. ANNUUS COMMON SUNFLOWER	Annual	1–12 ft./ 2 ft.	yellow, white, or bronze/summer	What would late summer be without them? Our favorite is 'Italian White'.
HELICHRYSUM. *Everlasting, immortelle. Compositae. Annual or perennial herbs, subshrubs, and shrubs native to warm areas of the Old World, especially southern Africa and Australia. Full sun; well-drained soil.*				
H. ITALICUM CURRY PLANT	8–10	1–2 ft./ 1–3 ft.	yellow/ summer	May be grown as an annual or potted specimen where they're not hardy.
H. PETIOLARE LICORICE PLANT	10	1–2 ft./ 4–5 ft.	insignificant/ summer	Chartreuse 'Limelight', variegated 'Splash', and the silver foliage of the species add flair to any container grouping.

Name	Hardiness Zones	Height/Spread	Flower Color/ Season of Bloom	Notes
HUMULUS. Hop. *Cannabidaceae. Rough-stemmed, twining perennial vines native to northern temperate regions. Sun or partial shade; fertile, well-drained soil.*				
H. JAPONICUS JAPANESE HOP	8–10	climber to 20 ft. or more	greenish/ summer, autumn	We grow this tender perennial as a self-sowing annual in our autumn border. 'Variegatus' is the variegated form.
H. LUPULUS HOP	3–9	climber to 25 ft.	yellow/ summer	'Aureum' has golden foliage but is reputedly hardy only to Zone 5. Effective for lighting up partially shaded areas.
HYSSOPUS. Hyssop. *Perennial herbs native to southern Europe and central Asia. Sun; well-drained soil.*				
H. OFFICINALIS HYSSOP	3–9	18–24 in./ 24–36 in.	purplish blue/ late summer	'Albus' has white flowers.
INULA. *Compositae. Mostly perennial herbs and subshrubs native to Old World temperate and subtropical regions. Most species need sun, ordinary well-drained soil.*				
I. HELENIUM ELECAMPANE	3–9	10 ft./ 6–10 ft.	yellow/ midsummer to midautumn	Performs well in partial shade; a coarse plant for backgrounds.
LAMINUM. Dead nettle. *Lamiaceae. Annual or perennial herbs native to the Mediterranean region. Partial or full shade; moist but well-drained soil.*				
L. ALBUM, WHITE DEAD NETTLE, ARCHANGEL, SNOWFLAKE	3–9	6–24 in./ 24–36 in.	white/spring	A quietly handsome addition to our sunken garden.
L. GALEOBDOLON YELLOW ARCHANGEL	4–9	8–15 in./ 24–36 in.	yellow/ spring	'Herman's Pride', with silver-flecked dark green leaves, pairs well with leopard's-bane.
L. MACULATUM SPOTTED DEAD NETTLE	4–9	8 in./ 36 in.	pink or white/ late spring and early summer	'Beacon Silver', 'Shell Pink', 'White Nancy', and 'Pink Pewter' are fine cultivars, but you may get seedlings with their own distinctive leaves and flower colors.
LAURUS. Laurel. *Lauraceae. Evergreen trees and shrubs native to southern Europe, the Canary Islands, and the Azores. Sun; moisture-retentive but well-drained soil.*				
L. NOBILIS BAY LAUREL	8–10	10–50 ft./ 30 ft.	cream-yellow/ spring	A good container plant in colder regions.
LAVANDULA. Lavender. *Lamiaceae. Aromatic evergreen herbs and shrubs native to the Mediterranean region, Middle East, and India. Sun; well-drained soil.*				
L. ANGUSTIFOLIA ENGLISH LAVENDER	5–10	12–24 in./ 18–36 in.	lavender-blue, pink, or white/ summer	Pleasing partners of dwarf scabious such as 'Pink Mist', pinks, and 'Silver Carpet' lamb's-ears.
L. DENTATA FRINGED LAVENDER	8–10	2–3 ft./ 2–3 ft.	dark blue/ summer	This makes a fine container plant with fancy-leaved geraniums and verbenas.
L. MULTIFIDA BRANCHED LAVENDER	8–10	12–24 in./ 24–30 in.	violet-blue/ summer	We grow this interestingly-textured lavender on the patio.
L. STOECHAS STICK-A-DOVE LAVENDER	8–10	1–3 ft./ 1–3 ft.	rosy lavender or white / summer	Mexican fleabane and Mexican evening primrose make good companions for this lavender.
L. × INTERMEDIA LAVANDIN	5–10	1–4 ft./ 1–3 ft.	blue, violet, or pink/summer	Hybrids between *L. angustifolia* and *L. latifolia* include 'Alba', 'Grappenhill', 'Grosso', 'Provence', and 'Twickel Purple'.

Name	Hardiness Zones	Height/Spread	Flower Color/ Season of Bloom	Notes
LIATRIS. *Blazing-star. Compositae. Perennial herbs native to North America. Sun; moderately fertile, well-drained soil.*				
L. PUNCTATA WESTERN SNAKEROOT	4–9	1–2 ft./1 ft.	mauve pink/ summer	Drought tolerant and effective in western rock gardens.
L. PYCNOSTACHYA BUTTON SNAKEROOT	4–9	4 ft./1–2 ft.	mauve pink/ summer	Strong vertical accents that cure the late-season garden blahs.
L. SPICATA, KANSAS GAYFEATHER	4–9	2–3 ft./2 ft.	purplish pink/ late summer	Great with a carpet of nasturtiums at its feet.
LINUM. *Flax. Linaceae. Annual, biennial, or perennial herbs and shrubs native to northern temperate regions. Sun; well-drained soil.*				
L. PERENNE SUBSP. *LEWISII,* PRAIRIE FLAX	5–9	18 in./ 12–18 in.	sky blue/late spring and summer	Our hell strip is a cloud of soft blue, punctuated by silver partridge feather and pink dianthus in early summer; we cut the flax back halfway for another show in August.
MARRUBIUM. *Horehound. Lamiaceae. Aromatic perennial herbs native to temperate Eurasia. Sun; well-drained soil.*				
M. ROUNDIFOLIUM SILVER-EDGED HOREHOUND	4–10	10–18 in./ 15–30 in.	pale lavender/ early summer	A beauty tumbling down a rocky slope or the edge of the border.
M. VULGARE WHITE HOREHOUND	4–10	24 in./24 in.	white/ summer	We learned the hard way to keep this self-sower deadheaded.
MENTHA. *Mint Lamiaceae. Aromatic, chiefly perennial herbs native to temperate Eurasia and Africa. Sun (partial shade for variegated forms); moist soil. Extremely invasive.*				
M. SUAVEOLENS PINEAPPLE MINT	6–10	16–48 in./ indefinite	lilac, mauve, or white/summer	An interesting addition to our vegetable garden even though it runs around too much; variegated foliage available.
M. REQUIENII CORSICAN MINT	7–10	¼–4 in./ indefinite	lilac/ summer	Keeping this mint moist is worth it when you catch the eye-opening aroma of the crushed leaves.
M. SPICATA SPEARMINT	4–10	1–3 ft./ indefinite	lilac, pink, or white/summer	Like peppermint, it's suitable only for a confined space or the straightjacket of a pot.
MONARDA. *Wild bergamot, horsemint. Lamiaceae. Aromatic annual or perennial herbs native to North America. Sun; M. didyma can be invasive in rich, moist soil.*				
M. CITRIODORA LEMON MINT	Annual	2–4 ft./ 1–2 ft	purplish pink/ summer	Save seed from the most richly colored flowers to develop a showy strain.
M. DIDYMA BEE BALM OSWEGO TEA	4–10	16–48 in./ 12–24 in.	pink, red, or purple/summer	We refuse to even discuss the mildew problem inherent in some cultivars; we tell visitors we grow the rare silver-leaved form.
M. PUNCTATA HORSEMINT	3–10	2–4 ft./ 1–2 ft.	yellow with purple spots/ summer and autumn	An intriguing plant that behaves as an annual for us.
M. FISTULOSA WILD BERGAMOT	3–9	4–6 ft./ 2–5 ft.	Lilac to pink/ summer and autumn	The cultivars 'Prairie Night' and 'Violet Queen' stay mildew-free for us but not for everyone. They make good compost if we're wrong.
MYRRHIS. *Sweet cicely. Umbelliferae. Aromatic perennial herb native to Europe. Sun or dappled shade; moist soil. Deadhead to prevent reseeding.*				
M. ODORATA SWEET CICELY	3–9	2–4 ft./ 1–3 ft.	white/late spring	A pretty, airy plant that makes everything around it look even better.

Name	Hardiness Zones	Height/Spread	Flower Color/ Season of Bloom	Notes
MYRTUS. Myrtle. *Myrtaceae. Aromatic evergreen shrubs native to the Mediterranean region and northern Africa. Sun; moderately fertile soil. In cold climates, grow in pots.*				
M. COMMUNIS MYRTLE	9–10	3–15 ft./ 3–10 ft	white/spring and summer	We especially like the variegated form as a container plant.
NEPETA. Catmint. *Lamiaceae. Chiefly perennial herbs native to Eurasia, northern Africa, and the mountains of tropical Africa. Sun; well-drained soil.*				
N. × *FAASSENII* BLUE CATMINT	4–10	12–18 in./ 24–36 in.	lavender blue/ June and July	We've never met a catmint we didn't like.
N. PHYLLOCLAMYS	5–10	6 in./12 in.	blue/summer	A must for the western gardener who enjoys silver plants. Good in rock gardens.
N. SIBIRICA	4–10	3 ft./ indefinite	blue/summer	One of our favorite perennials for the color and duration of the flowers, even if we have to excuse its rambling ways.
OCIMUM. Basil. *Lamiaceae. Aromatic annual of perennial herbs and shrubs native to the Old World Tropics. Sun; good garden soil. Grown for its foliage; flowers insignificant.*				
O. BASILICUM SWEET BASIL	Annual	8–24 in./ 6–24 in.	white/summer	The most ornamental are 'African Blue' and 'Red Rubin', but all cultivars show qualities as distinctive as their tastes.
ORIGANUM. Oregano, marjoram. *Lamiaceae. Perennial herbs and subshrubs native to Eurasia. Sun; well-drained soil.*				
O. DICTAMNUS DITTANY OF CRETE	8–10	5–6 in./ 16 in.	tiny flowers within large pink bracts/summer	A conspicuous container plant in colder regions.
O. LAEVIGATUM GREEK OREGANO	5–10	10–30 in./ 36 in.	purplish pink/ August to September	'Herrenhausen' and 'Hopleys' are stunning in late summer.
O. VULGARE OREGANO WILD MARJORAM	5–10	12–30 in./ 12–30 in.	white to dark pink/summer and early autumn	Golden and variegated cultivars may be less hardy than the species.
PELARGONIUM. Geranium. *Geraniaceae. Annual or perennial herbs and subshrubs native chiefly to southern Africa but also to tropical Africa, the Middle East, and Australia. Sun; well-drained soil. In cold regions, grow in pots.*				
P. SPP.	9–10	Highly variable	orange, pink, red, white/ summer	It's almost unthinkable that we wouldn't display dozens of fancy-leaf and scented geraniums on the patio.
PERILLA. Perilla. *Chinese basil, Shisho, Lamiaceae. Annual herbs native from India to Japan.*				
P. FRUTESCENS	Annual	2–4 ft./ 1–2 ft.	white/ summer	'Atropurpurea', with bronze nearly metallic looking leaves, self-sows in many of our borders and even in our patio containers.
PETROSELINUM. Parsley, *Umbelliferae. Biennial herbs native to Europe.*				
P. CRISPUM	6–10	1–3 ft./ 1–2 ft.	yellow/ summer, the second year	The flat-leaf Italian parsley (var. *neapolitanum*) is our favorite for both cooking and edging in the vegetable garden.
PLECTRANTHUS. Swedish ivy. *Lamiaceae. Annual or perennial herbs or shrubs native to Africa, Asia, and Australia. Sun to partial shade; moderately fertile soil.*				
P. ARGENTATUS	10	2 ft./2 ft.	inconspicuous white/summer, autumn	A great container plant valued for its slightly puckered silver leaves and upright habit.

Name	Hardiness Zones	Height/Spread	Flower Color/ Season of Bloom	Notes
P. FORSTERI CUBAN OREGANO	10	8–24 in./ 10–24 in.	white to pale mauve/summer, autumn	The variegated leaves enliven container planting like nobody's business.

POLYGONUM. *Knotweed. Polygonaceae. Mostly annual or perennial herbs native to northern temperate regions. Sun or partial shade; moderately fertile soil. Many are very invasive.*

Name	Hardiness Zones	Height/Spread	Flower Color/ Season of Bloom	Notes
P. AUBERTII SILVER LACE VINE	5–9	climber to 40 ft. or more	white or greenish/ summer–autumn	For covering unsightly fences and structures, maybe neighborhoods.

PRIMULA. *Primrose. Primulaceae. Perennial herbs native chiefly to northern temperate regions. Partial shade; moist but well-drained soil.*

Name	Hardiness Zones	Height/Spread	Flower Color/ Season of Bloom	Notes
P. DENTICULATA DRUMSTICK PRIMROSE	5–8	12–14 in./ 12–18 in.	bright pink, rose, or white/spring	In our garden, the cute little lollipops often emerge too early and get nipped by frost.
P. ELATIOR OXLIP	3–8	6–12 in./ 6 in.	yellow/ spring	The easiest and perhaps most rewarding primrose for those who don't live in ideal "primrose country".
P. VERIS COWSLIP	5–9	6–8 in./ 6–8 in.	yellow with orange markings/spring	Another easy primrose that shines with companions like forget-me-nots and violas.
P. VULGARIS ENGLISH PRIMROSE	5–9	6 in./ 10 in.	pale yellow/late winter and spring	A good doer that doesn't need the pampering that the hybrid polyanthus types do.

PRUNELLA. *Self-heal. Lamiaceae. Sprawling perennial herbs native to Eurasia, northern Africa, and North America. Sun or partial shade; moderately moist soil.*

Name	Hardiness Zones	Height/Spread	Flower Color/ Season of Bloom	Notes
P. GRANDIFLORA SELF-HEAL	5–9	4–6 in./ 12 in.	pink, lavender, or white/late spring	Not a stellar floral display but we appreciate it more and more in partial shade.
P. LACINIATA	4–9	1 ft./2 ft.	mauve-pink/ late spring	Attractive dissected foliage makes it a good choice for partial shade in front of bleeding-hearts.

PULMONARIA. *Lungwort. Boraginaceae. Hairy perennial herbs native to Europe, Asia, and western United States. Partial shade; moist soil.*

Name	Hardiness Zones	Height/Spread	Flower Color/ Season of Bloom	Notes
P. SACCHARATA BETHLEHEM SAGE; *P. LONGIFOLIA*	4–9	1 ft./2 ft.	pink turning to blue/spring	Favorites of ours include deep blue–flowered 'Benediction'; 'Excalibur', with silver-splashed leaves; and heavily silvered 'Roy Davidson'.

RHEUM. *Rhubarb. Polygonaceae. Stout perennial herbs native to Eurasia. Sun to partial shade; moist but well-drained soil.*

Name	Hardiness Zones	Height/Spread	Flower Color/ Season of Bloom	Notes
R. PALMATUM CHINESE RHUBARB	5–9	6 ft./3 ft.	deep red/ late spring	A foliage focal point and a spectacle when blooming; ours grows best with afternoon shade on their huge leaves.

ROSMARINUS. *Rosemary. Lamiaceae. Evergreen shrubs native to southern Europe and northern Africa. Full sun; well-drained soil.*

Name	Hardiness Zones	Height/Spread	Flower Color/ Season of Bloom	Notes
R. OFFICINALIS ROSEMARY	7–10	1–6 ft/includes creepers and tall hedge-forming plants	blue, pink, or white/spring, summer	The many forms and colors extend the options in borders, cottage gardens, and containers.

RUTA. *Rue. Rutaceae. Aromatic or pungent perennial herbs or subshrubs native from the Mediterranean region to western Asia. Sun to partial shade; well-drained soil. Sap of R. graveolens can cause photodermatitis.*

Name	Hardiness Zones	Height/Spread	Flower Color/ Season of Bloom	Notes
R. GRAVEOLENS RUE	4–10	24 in./18 in.	yellow/ summer	'Jackman's Blue' has the bluest foliage; 'Variegata' has cream-edged foliage.

Name	Hardiness Zones	Height/Spread	Flower Color/ Season of Bloom	Notes
SALVIA. Sage. Lamiaceae. Annual, biennial, or perennial herbs, subshrubs, or shrubs; cosmopolitan. Sun; well-drained soil.				
S. ARGENTEA SILVER CLARY SILVER SAGE	5–9	24–36 in./ 18 in.	white/ summer	The silver, hairy rosettes of leaves beg for dramatic pairings with ornamental grasses and bronze-leaved sage; much longer lived if grown lean and dry.
S. CLEVELANDII CLEVELAND SAGE BLUE SAGE	9–10	18–36 in./ 12–20 in.	blue, violet, or white/summer	To us the leaves smell like hand lotion. A good container plant but dies if overwatered.
S. FORSKAOHLEI	5–9	3–4 ft./ 2–3 ft.	purple/summer	Several shows are possible if the plants are cut well back after the June flowering.
S. GLUTINOSA JUPITER'S DISTAFF	5–9	3 ft./2 ft.	butter yellow/ summer	Not everyone's cup of tea, but we enjoy it amid Russian sage and liatris.
S. GUARANITICA	5–10	4–7 ft/ 2–3 ft.	blue/late summer	'Black and Blue' is a popular cultivar.
S. INVOLUCRATA ROSY-LEAF SAGE	9–10	5–7 ft./2 ft.	pink/autumn	'Bethellii' has flowers slightly reminiscent of rose buds.
S. LEUCANTHA MEXICAN BUSH SAGE	9–10	2 ft./2 ft.	white with violet calyx/ summer–autumn	A brilliant long show from an adaptable plant; we enjoy it in pots.
S. OFFICINALIS GARDEN SAGE	5–9	12–36 in./ 18–36 in.	purple-blue/ summer	The variegated and bronze cultivars offer many options for interesting combinations, even if nobody actually needs this much sage.
S. PATENS	7–9	18–24 in./ 18 in.	gentian blue/ late summer and autumn	A fabulous color that perks up our borders late in the season.
S. ELEGANS PINEAPPLE SAGE	7–10	3–5 ft./3 ft.	ruby red/late summer	Glorious in the South but our show is often ruined by early frost.
S. SCLAREA CLARY SAGE	4–9	3 ft./2 ft.	mauve-pink bracts/summer	'Turkestanica' is bigger, bolder, and brighter.
S. VIRIDIS	Annual	18 in./12 in.	pink, white, or violet bracts/ summer	Self-sows reliably for us; purple tone is a good foil for many lilies and daylilies.
SAMBUCUS. Elder. Caprifoliaceae: Perennial herbs, shrubs, and small trees native to temperate and subtropical regions worldwide. Sun or partial shade; rich, moist soil.				
S. NIGRA	3–9	15–30 ft./ 11–15 ft.	white/late spring	'Guincho Purple' has bronze foliage; 'Marginatus' is yellow variegated: 'Aureus' is golden. All have black berries.
SANGUINARIA. Bloodroot. Papaveraceae. Perennial woodland herb native to eastern North America. Sun or partial shade; humus-rich, well-drained soil.				
S. CANDADENSIS	3–8	6–24 in./ 12–18 in.	pink or white/ spring	Few plants cause as much excitement in our spring garden as the double form; the single form flowers slightly later and—though pretty—is rather anticlimactic.
SANGUISORBA. Burnet. Rosaceae. Perennial herbs or small shrubs native to northern temperate regions. Sun or partial shade; moist soil.				
S. CANADENSIS CANADIAN BURNET	3–8	4–6 ft./2 ft.	white/late summer and autumn	Stands out in autumn groupings with ornamental grasses, asters, and Japanese anemones.

Name	Hardiness Zones	Height/Spread	Flower Color/ Season of Bloom	Notes
S. OFFICINALIS GREAT BURNET	4–8	12–42 in./ 9–24 in.	maroon/ summer	Needs deadheading to prevent reseeding; effective with pinks.

SANTOLINA. *Lavender cotton. Compositae. Aromatic evergreen shrubs native to the Mediterranean region. Sun; well-drained soil essential.*

Name	Hardiness Zones	Height/Spread	Flower Color/ Season of Bloom	Notes
S. CHAMAECYPARISSUS LAVENDER COTTON	5–10	6–20 in./ 12–24 in.	yellow/summer	Great behind fall-blooming colchicums; 'Lemon Queen', 'Nana', and 'Pretty Carol' have silver foliage.
S. ROSMARINIFOLIA	5–10	2 ft./3 ft.	bright yellow/ midsummer	Fine-textured foliage is effective with yuccas.

SAPONARIA. *Soapwort. Caryophyllaceae. Annual or perennial herbs native chiefly to the Mediterranean region. Sun; well-drained soil.*

Name	Hardiness Zones	Height/Spread	Flower Color/ Season of Bloom	Notes
S. OCYMOIDES ROCK SOAPWORT	4–8	12–24 in./ 16–30 in.	pale pink to crimson/June and July	In most respects, a dryland gardener's dream, although its seeding may turn into a nightmare.
S. OFFICINALIS SOAPWORT BOUNCING BET	2–8	24 in./ indefinite	pale pink/late spring to early autumn	Too invasive for most small gardens; a variegated form is slightly less vigorous.

SILYBUM. *Milk thistle. Compositae. Thistlelike annual or biennial herbs native to the Mediterranean region. Sun; well-drained fertile soil.*

Name	Hardiness Zones	Height/Spread	Flower Color/ Season of Bloom	Notes
S. MARIANUM MILK THISTLE	7–10	3–4 ft./ 1–3 ft.	lavender or white/summer	Gorgeous silver-patterned rosettes of leaves add pizzazz to our white-and-silver border.

SMYRNIUM. *Alexanders. Umbelliferae. Biennial herbs native to western Europe and the Mediterranean region. Sun; moist but well-drained soil.*

Name	Hardiness Zones	Height/Spread	Flower Color/ Season of Bloom	Notes
S. PERFOLIATUM ALEXANDERS	5–10	2–3 ft./ 1 ft.	lime-chartreuse/ spring	The small but brilliant flowers highlight spring bulbs.

STACHYS. *Betony. Lamiaceae. Annual or perennial herbs, subshrubs, and shrubs native to temperate and subtropical regions and tropical mountains. Sun or partial shade; well-drained soil.*

Name	Hardiness Zones	Height/Spread	Flower Color/ Season of Bloom	Notes
S. BYZANTINA LAMB'S EARS	4–9	12–30 in./ indefinite	pink/summer	'Helene von Stein' ('Big Ears') offers larger leaves; 'Phantom' has variegated foliage; 'Primrose Heron' is chartreuse; nonblooming 'Silver Carpet' is a valued edging plant.
S. GRANDIFLORA	5–9	2–4 ft./ 2 ft.	lavender-pink/ summer	The showiest of the bunch, we grow it in partial shade.
S. OFFICINALIS WOOD BETONY	4–8	15–30 in./ 18–30 in.	magenta, pink, or white/summer	Lovely with garden sage and lady's bedstraw.

SYMPHYTUM. *Comfrey. Boraginaceae. Perennial herbs native from Europe to the Caucasus and Iran.*

Name	Hardiness Zones	Height/Spread	Flower Color/ Season of Bloom	Notes
S. × UPLANDICUM RUSSIAN COMFREY	4–9	2–3 ft./ 2–3 ft.	pink or blue/ late spring and early summer	'Variegatum', with white–and cream–edged leaves, is one of the most beautiful foliage plants but still difficult to obtain.

TANACETUM. *Tansy. Compositae. Mostly aromatic annual or perennial herbs and subshrubs native to northern temperate regions. Sun or partial shade; well-drained soil.*

Name	Hardiness Zones	Height/Spread	Flower Color/ Season of Bloom	Notes
T. BALSAMITA COSTMARY	4–8	3–4 ft./ 2–4 ft.	white/ late summer	Small daisies have an old-fashioned charm; var. *tomentosum* has aromatic leaves.
T. DENSUM VAR. AMANI PARTRIDGE FEATHER	5–8	10 in./ 12–36 in.	yellow/summer	Much hardier than most references indicate if given sharp drainage. A valued feature in our hell strip.

Name	Hardiness Zones	Height/Spread	Flower Color/ Season of Bloom	Notes
T. NIVEUM SNOW DAISY	5–8	2 ft./2 ft.	white/summer	A new western favorite that tolerates drought but rots out in the east; let a few plants self-sow.
T. PARTHENIUM FEVERFEW	4–9	8–36 in./ 8–24 in.	white or yellow/summer	The golden form 'Aureum' has become our favorite for almost any situation in sun or shade.

TEUCRIUM. *Germander. Lamiaceae. Mostly perennial herbs, subshrubs, and shrubs; cosmopolitan. Sun; well-drained soil.*

Name	Hardiness Zones	Height/Spread	Flower Color/ Season of Bloom	Notes
T. CHAMAEDRYS WALL GERMANDER	5–9	4–8 in./ 10–24 in.	purplish pink/ summer and autumn	Pretty mounds when in flower for edging; variegated foliage.

THYMUS. *Thyme. Lamiaceae. Aromatic perennial herbs and subshrubs native to Eurasia. Sun; well-drained soil.*

Name	Hardiness Zones	Height/Spread	Flower Color/ Season of Bloom	Notes
T. × CITRIODORUS LEMON THYME	5–9	4–6 in./ 24 in.	pink/late spring	'Argenteus' has showy golden foliage; 'Variegatus' tends to revert to green.
T. PRAECOX SUBSP. *ARCTICUS* 'COCCINEUS' CRIMSON THYME	4–8	½–3 in./ 36 in.	magenta/late spring	Red-flowered 'Coccineus' is effectively paired with Sedum 'Vera Jameson'.
T. P. SUBSP. *A.* 'LANUGINOSUS' WOOLLY THYME	4–8	½ in./ 18–40 in.	pink/summer	The best thyme for paths or edging in partial shade.
T. P. SUBSP. *A* 'MINUS'	4–8	½–3 in./ 36 in.	pink/late spring	This tiny thyme works in small cracks between paving stones.

TROPAEOLUM. *Nasturtium. Tropaeolaceae. Annual and perennial herbs native from Mexico to Patagonia. Sun; well-drained ordinary soil.*

Name	Hardiness Zones	Height/Spread	Flower Color/ Season of Bloom	Notes
T. MAJUS NASTURTIUM	Annual	10–48 in./ 12–24 in., more for trailers.	red, orange, or yellow/summer	Alaska hybrids have variegated leaves that look great combined with cabbage, tomatoes, or lemon grass.

VALERIANA. *Valerian. Valerianaceae. Perennial herbs, subshrubs, and shrubs native to all continents except Australia. Sun or partial shade; moist soil.*

Name	Hardiness Zones	Height/Spread	Flower Color/ Season of Bloom	Notes
V. OFFICINALIS VALERIAN, GARDEN HELIOTROPE	5–9	4–5 ft./ 2 ft.	white or pink/ summer	We select seedlings for early-season bronze leaves that fade to green in summer.
V. PHU	5–9	15 in./ 12–15 in.	white/summer	'Aurea' has yellow-green leaves in spring that light up partially shaded beds.

VERBASCUM. *Mullein. Scrophulariaceae. Mostly biennial herbs native to Asia and Europe; some naturalized in North America. Sun, well-drained soil. Many flowers close in afternoon.*

Name	Hardiness Zones	Height/Spread	Flower Color/ Season of Bloom	Notes
V. BOMBYCIFERUM SILVER MULLEIN	5–9	4–6 ft./ 2–3 ft.	yellow/summer	'Arctic Summer' is noted for its extra-silver foliage. We transplant or give away the seedlings.
V. CHAIXII	5–9	3 ft./2 ft.	yellow or white/ summer	'Album' is white with a plum center; deadhead to prevent reseeding.
V. THAPSUS MINER'S CANDLE	5–9	4–8 ft./2 ft.	yellow/summer	Weedy but dramatic; deadhead for sure.
V. WIDEMANNIANUM	5–10	2–3 ft./1 ft.	purple/summer	Hard to find but worth the search; must have perfect winter drainage.

SUBJECT INDEX

Italic page numbers indicate photographs.

A

Abscess root, 83
Abutilon, 125
Acanthus, 73
Adam's needle, 62, 106
Agapanthus, 96
Agastache, 100
Agave, 102, 106, 120
Alaska cedar, 79
Alexanders, 16
Alkanet, 70, 83
Allium, 42–43
Aloe, 90, 106
Amaranth, 60, 68, 74, 102
American pennyroyal, 84
Anchusa, 3
Anemone, 62
Anise basil, 122
Anise hyssop, 100
Anise, 83
Annuals, 60
Apache plume, 103
Apple mint, 57
Apple, 47, 115
Aquatic plants, 81
Armenian cranesbill, 3
Artemisia, 7, 12, 17, 22–23, 24, 55, 63–64, 74, 94, 100, 127, 129
Artichoke, 30, 48
Arugula, 47–48
Aster, 39, 71, 74
Autumn border, 72–74
Autumn crocus, 118
Avena grass, 16, 65
Azalea, 85
Aztec herb, 126

B

Baby's breath, 42–43, 53, 59
Baby's tears, 112
Bachelor button, 40, 54, 102
Ballota, 18
Bamboo, 122
Banana, 68, 90
Barberry, 16, 23, 123, 128
Basil, 12, 20, 21, 40, 44, 47–48, 60, 120, 122, 126
Bay, 106
Bean, 4, 40
Beasley, Jeof, 68
Bee balm, 40, 56, 69, 89
Bella Madrona, 68
Bellflower, 19, 34, 40, 61, 65
Bergenia, 82, 118
Bindweed, 95
Bishop's weed, 33
Bistort, 17, 86, 89
Blackberry lily, 74
Bleeding heart, 9, 87

Blood grass, 23
Blue basil, 127
Blue willow, 88
Boneset, 72
Borage, 42–43, 60
Borders, 49–74: annual additions, 60; autumn border, 72–74; classics, 60–71; color, 52–56; spacing, 59–60; textural herbs, 56–59; water-wise, 97–100
Bougainvillea, 96, 101
Bowman's root, 83
Box knot, 123
Boxwood, 36, 47
Bronze foliage, 19–23
Bronze-leaf elder, 23
Broom, 105
Brunnera, 85
Buff-and-olive, 100
Bugleweed, 84
Bush basil, 125

C

Cabbage, 47, 99
Cactus, 50, 103, 120
Calamint, 84, 118
California bay, 106
California laurel, 106
California poppy, 95, 101
California sagebrush, 26
Calla lily, 96
Campanula, 118
Campion, 112
Canadian burnet, 60, 71–72
Canna, 19, 39, 90
Caper bush, 90
Cardamom, 90
Cardoon, 30, 48, 56, 97
Carpet bugle, 115
Castor bean, 23, 40, 56, 60, 90
Catchfly, 112
Catmint, 19, 29, 65, 73, 102
Celandine poppy, 83
Century plant, 106
Chamisa, 102
Chamomile, 26
Chervil, 80
Chives, 40, 44, 47, 56, 101, 127
Chokeberry, 88
Circle flower, 133
Clary sage, 64, 100
Cleome, 39
Cliff rose, 103
Cobweb houseleek, 112
Cockleshell bellflower, 117
Colchicum, 80
Coleus, 20, 63, 81
Color, in border, 52–56; in foliage, 11–36
Columbine, 76, 115, 118
Comfrey, 85
Coneflower, 49, 54, 60, 67,

72, 74, 89, 102
Corsican mint, 88, 112
Corsican pansy, 117
Cosmos, 40, 45
Costmary, 63
Cottage garden, 37–48
Cow parsnip, 9, 78
Cowboy's fried eggs, 95
Cowslip, 115
Coyote mint, 105
Cranesbill, 57, 74, 80, 108
Creeping oregano, 122
Crocus, 26, 117
Cuban oregano, 48, 56, 122, 126
Culinary herbs, 5, 122, 127
Curry plant, 24, 29, 62, 106
Cyclamen, 25, 118

D

Daffodil, 76, 80
Dahlia, 22–23, 39, 64
Dandelion, 95
Daphne, 36, 39
Daylily, 37, 40, 44, 56, 113
Dead nettle, 117–118
Delphinium, 28, 50, 61, 66, 99
Desert spoon, 94
Dianthus, 19, 26, 51, 111
Dill, 44, 47, 60, 74
Dillon, Helen, 32
Dog fennel, 18
Dogwood, 74, 75, 79, 87
Doku-dami, 88
Double bird's-foot trefoil, 112
Dracaena, 23
Drought-tolerant herbs, 5, 97–100
Drumstick primrose, 80
Dryland garden, 91–106: blossoms, 100–102; hell strip, 92, 94–97; Mediterranean influence, 106; water-wise border, 97–100; woodies, 102–106;
Dunesilver, 10, 26
Dusty miller, 21, 31, 64, 119

E

Echinacea, 90
Eddleman, Edith, 18
Elder, 36
English daisy, 112
English lavender, 69
English primrose, 79
Ephedra, 105
Evening primrose, 40, 113

F

Fairies' thimble, 117
Fancy-leaf geranium, 32–33
Felicia, 11
Fennel, 20, 48, 56, 60, 74

Fern, 77, 79, 118
Fernbush, 102
Feverfew, 9, 15, 28, 61, 62–63, 115
Fibrous begonia, 35
Finnis, Valerie, 18
Fleabane, 37, 96
Foliage, 11–36: bronze, 19–23; gold, 12–19; silver, 23–31; variegated, 31–36
Forget-me-not, 89, 118
Fountain grass, 7, 128
Four-square garden, 40, 47–48
Foxglove, 19, 59, 78, 80, 100
Fuchsia, 131

G

Garlic chives, 73, 101
Garlic, 10, 35, 41, 101
Gayfeather, 98, 100
Gentian, 116
Geranium, 126
Geum, 34, 133
Ginger, 9, 57, 79, 122
Globe thistle, 37, 53, 54
Goat's rue, 66, 70
Golden comfrey, 6, 12, 15
Golden feverfew, 9, 15
Golden hops, 3, 12, 14, 15, 17
Golden lemon balm, 15
Golden moneywort, 9
Golden oregano, 15, 122
Golden thyme, 15
Golden valerian, 12
Grape hyacinth, 82
Grecian foxglove, 100
Greek yarrow, 18, 95, 112

H

Hardiman, Lucy, 128
Hawks, Kim, 18
Headache tree, 106
Heartleaf, 84
Hedge woundwort, 118
Heliotrope, 123
Hell strip, 92, 94–97
Hemlock, 79
Hens-and-chicks, 117–118
Herb Robert, 74, 80
Hogan, Sean, 24, 94
Holly, 36, 47, 79
Honesty, 80, 84
Hops, 3, 12, 14, 17, 38, 59
Horehound, 37
Horned poppy, 99
Horsemint, 69
Horsetail, 88
Hosta, 9, 77, 84, 85, 86
Hot housemaid, 64
Hyacinth, 82
Hydrangea, 80
Hypertufa pots, 124
Hyssop, 74, 102

I

Ice plant, 95, *113*, 120
Impatiens, 81, *131*
Indian blanket, *28*, 96
Indian physic, 84
Iris, 35, 40, 44, 47, 52, *57*, 76, *82*, 95, 101, 111
Irish moss, 15, 115
Italian basil, 20
Italian basil, 122
Ivy, *83*, 115

J

Jacob's ladder, 79, *83*, 83
Jasmine, 96
Jerusalem sage, 60, 100
Joe-pye weed, 20, *58*, *71*, 72, *73*, 89
Johnny-jump-up, 26, 117
Joy Creek Nursery, 62
Juniper, 59, 105, 130
Jupiter's beard, 19–20, 40, *49*, *63*, *68*, 70, 102
Jupiter's distaff, 66, *98*

K

Kelaidis, Panayoti, 117
Kellerer's yarrow, 68
Kidney vetch, 101
Knapweed, *54*

L

Labrador violet, 117
Lady's bedstraw, 16, *63*
Lady's mantle, 16, *19*, 36, 40, *63*, 77, 108, *113*, 117
Lamb's ears, *14*, 18, *28*, 33, 36, *63*, 74, *82*, *91*, *109*, *133*
Lamb's quarters, 95
Lamium, 12, *83*
Larkspur, 65
Lavandins, 69
Lavender cotton, 60, 69
Lavender, *17*, 23, *28*, *40*, *42–43*, 62, *63*, 101, 106
Lead plant, 102
Lebanese oregano, 64, *116*
Lemon grass, 15, 74, 123
Lemon mint, 48, 69, *97*
Lemon thyme, 34, 111
Lemon verbena, 122
Leopard's bane, 80
Lettuce, *48*
Licorice plant, 18, 30, *126*, *131*
Ligularia, *131*
Lilac, 38, 80
Lily of the valley, *17*
Lilyturf, 15
Lion's ear, 74
Lobelia, 89, 117, *126*
Longview Farm, 39
Loosestrife, 20
Lotus vine, *119*

Lovage, 18
Love-in-a-mist, *16*, 40, 102
Love-lies-bleeding, *45*
Lungwort, *82*, 85

M

Madagascar periwinkle, 90
Magnolia, *85*
Mallow, *110*
Maltese cross, *28*
Mandevilla, 128
Mandrake, 90
Manzanita, 103
Marguerite daisy, *131*
Marigold, 48, 88, *128*, 128
Marsh marigold, 88
Marsh woundwort, 88
Meadow clary, 100
Meadow sage, 64
Mediterranean influence, 106
Mexican bush sage, 30, *51*, 67, 96, 101
Mexican fleabane, *60*, 101
Miner's candle, 99
Mint, *41*, 123
Mock strawberry, 118
Monarda, 20
Money plant, 84
Moneywort, 16, 115
Mormon tea, 105
Morning glory, *4*, 48, 59
Mount Atlas daisy, 95, 112
Mountain sandwort, 112
Mullein, *10*, *37*, 99
Mustard, *4*
Myrtle, 63

N

Narcissus, 118
Nasturtium, 15, 40, *44*, *48*, 60, 74, 96, 102
New Zealand flax, 23, 36, 90, 122
Nicotiana, 60, 62
Nooks/crannies, 107–118
Nutmeg, 90

O

Oat grass, 35
Ocotillo, 106
Okra, *55*, 62
Oleander, 120, 128
Opium poppy, 31, 48, 60
Orach, 12, 20, 60
Oregano, 15, 57, 59, 73, 100, 108, 127
Ornamental grass, 38
Ornamental pepper, 64
Oswego tea, 69
Oxlip, 79, 115

P

Palm, 90, *129*
Parsley, 47, 127

Partridge feather, 23, 56, *70*, 73, 95
Path plants, 111–114
Pear, 47
Pearly everlasting, 24, 72, *74*
Pelargonium, 33, 90
Pennyroyal, 88
Penstemons, *7*, 61, 128
Peppers, *22–23*
Peppermint, 128
Perilla, 12, 40, 60, *119*, *121*, *128*
Perlite, 124
Pesticide, 127
Phlox, *61*
Pincushion flower, 19
Pineapple sage, 67
Pinks, 26, 28–29, 40, 56, 95, 111
Plantain, 83
Plectranthus, *55*
Plume poppy, *39*
Pokeberry, 74
Poppy, *4*, *42–43*, 47, 74, *97*
Potassium, 127
Potato, 47
Potentilla, 56
Potted herbs, *119–131*
Potting mix, 124
Prairie sage, 24
Prairie snowball, 101
Prickly pear, 106
Prickly poppy, 95–96
Primrose path, 115–118
Primrose, 6, 83, 115
Prince's feather, 23
Princess flower, *129*
Prunella, *9*, 83, *133*
Pulmonaria, *6*, *9*
Purple sage, 20, 56, *62*
Pussy-toes, 111–112
Pussy willow, 88

Q

Quinine rose, 103

R

Rabbitbrush, 102
Rainbow bed, 55
Red valerian, 70
Reed, Joanna, 39
Reference chart, 133–146
Rhubarb, 80
River birch, 88
Rock soapwort, 101
Roman chamomile, 115
Roman wormwood, 24, *73*
Rose campion, *3*, *10*, 31, 62, 64, 102, *110*
Rose mallow, 63
Rose, 7, 44, 50, *128*
Rosemary, 106, *123*, *125*
Rue, *51*, *57*, 63, 66, 102
Russian comfrey, 34, *66*

Russian sage, *58*, *62*, *73*, *98*, 100

S

Sackville-West, Vita, 55
Saffron crocus, *70*, *73*, 101
Sage, 26, *44*, *60*, *63*, 64, 66–67, 100, 127
Salvia, 30, *61*, *65*, 66, *128*
Sampson, Jim, 68
Sand cherry, 23
Sandalwood, 90
Sanderson, Parker, 24, 94
Santolina, 23, 69, 73, *93*, 96, 101, 106
Savory, 102, 127
Scarlet runner bean, *4*
Scented geranium, 32–34, *35*, *41*, *119*, *121*
Scotch thistle, 99–100
Sea holly, *10*, *54*, *66*, *94*
Sea kale, *10*, 30, 99
Sea pinks, *63*, 111
Sedum, 56, *60*, *110*, 112, 117–118
Self-heal, 83, 117–118
Serbian yarrow, 112
Serviceberry, 105
Shade and stream, 75–90:
    marsh plants, 87–89;
    native plants, 76–79;
    spring plants, 79–81; sub-
    tropical plants, 89–90;
    summer plants, 81–84;
    variegated plants, 84–87;
Siberian pea shrub, 102
Silver centaurea, 39
Silver foliage, 23–31
Silver lotus, 35
Silver-edged horehound, 18, 26
Silvery clary, 34
Skunk cabbage, *86*, 88
Skunkbush, 105
Snakeroot, 100
Sneezewort, 68
Snow daisy, 63, 95
Soapweed, 106
Soapwort, *104*
Solomon's seal, 82
Sorrel, 47
Spanish butterfly, 70
Spanish cinquefoil, 112
Spanish sandwort, 112
Speedwell, 29
Spirea, 16, 102
Springer, Lauren, 5, 40, 47
St.-John's-wort, 36, 80, 83, 118
Stick-a-dove lavender, 70, *93*
Stock, *40*, 51
Straw yellow, 100
Strawberry, *4*, 34, *40*, 47–48, 74, *106*, 111, 115
Sumac, 47, 74, 105

Sunflower, 31, 40, 62, 74, *98*
Sweet Annie, 18, 48, 74
Sweet cicely, *17*, 80, 89
Sweet flag, 88
Sweet potato, 16, *22–23*, 64, *119*
Sweet William, 18, *28*, 111
Sweet woodruff, 80, 118

T

Tartarian dogwood, 88
Tatroe, Marcia and Randy, 29
Tennessee coneflower, 67
Texas bush sage, 105
Texas ranger, 105
Textural herbs, 56–59
Thyme, *11, 14, 44, 51, 60, 65, 107*, 108, *110*, 111, *113, 114*, 127
Tiarella, *83*
Toadflax, *61*, 100
Tulip, 118
Tunic flower, 95, 112
Turkish onion, 101
Turkish veronica, 112
Tweedia, 63

V

Valerian, 70
Variegated foliage, 31–36
Vegetable garden, 5, 44–48
Verbena, *119, 128*
Verey, Rosemary, *46*, 47, 122
Vermiculite, 124
Veronica, *49*, 108, *110*, 112
Vervain, 70, 89
Viburnum, 79
Voodoo lily, *121*, 122

W

Water-wise planting, 92, 95, 97–100
Wave Hill, 128–129
Wet spots, 87–88
White Garden, 55
Wild rose, 105
Winterfat, 102
Wisteria, 96
Wood betony, 16, *63*, 76
Woolly milfoil, 67
Woolly thyme, 64–65, 115
Woolly veronica, 112
Woolly yarrow, 112
Wormwood, 24

Y

Yarrow, *45, 49, 65*, 67–68, 112, *113, 133*
Yellow archangel, 80
Yellow rose of Texas, 105
Yellow-stem dogwood, 88
Yucca, 50, 74, 106

Z

Zebra grass, 35

SPECIES INDEX

A

Abronia fragrans, 101
Acacia, 90, 102
Achillea, 60, 67; *A. ageratifolia*, 18, 112; *A. clypeolata*, 67; *A. filipendulina*, 67; *A. millefolium*, 68, 112; *A. ptarmica*, *49*, 68; *A. serbica*, 112; *A. tomentosa*, 67, 112; *A. × kellereri*, 68; *A. × lewisii*, 67
Acorus calamus, 88; *A. gramineus*, 35
Aegopodium podagraria, 33
Agastache barberi, *58*, *98*, 100; *A. cana*, 100; *A. foeniculum*, 100; *A. rupestris*, 100
Agave americana, *103*, 106
Ajuga reptans, 84, 115
Alchemilla alpina, 117; *A. glaucescens*, 117; *A. mollis*, 16
Allium caeruleum, 101; *A. cernuum*, 111; *A. karataviense*, 101; *A. tuberosum*, 73, 101
Aloe vera, 106
Amaranthus hypochondriacus, 23
Amaryllis belladonna, 96
Amelanchier alnifolia, 105
Amorpha canescens, 102
Ampelopsis brevipedunculata, 36
Amsonia hubrectii, 74
Anacyclus pyrethrum var. *depressus*, 95, 112
Anaphalis margaritacea, 72; *A. triplinervis*, 72
Anchusa, 2, 70
Anemone × hybrida, 36
Antennaria parvifolia, 111; *A. rosea*, 111
Anthriscus cerefolium, 80; *A. sylvestris*, 19
Anthyllis vulneraria, 101
Arctostaphylos spp., 103
Arenaria montana, 112; *A. tetraquetra*, 112
Argemone platyceras, 95
Armeria maritima, 111
Armoracia rusticana, 34
Aronia arbutifolia, 36
Arrhenatherum elatius subsp. *tuberosum*, 35
Artemisia, *22–23*, 26, *49*, *53*, *61*, 61, 128–129; *A. aborescens*, 128; *A. abrotanum* var. *limoneum*, 18; *A. absinthium*, 24; *A. annua*, 18; *A. armeniaca*, 26; *A. californica*, 26; *A. frigida*, 26;

A. lactiflora 53; *A. ludoviciana*, 24; *A. pontica*, 24; *A. pycnocephala*, 26; *A. schmidtiana*, 24, 95; *A. stelleriana*, 26, 34
Asclepias tuberosa, 100–101
Astrantia major, 33
Atriplex hortensis, 20

B

Ballota, 16; *B. pseudodictamnus*, 18
Belamcanda chinensis, 74
Betula nigra, 88
Brunnera macrophylla, 80, 84

C

Calamintha grandiflora, 33, 84; *C. nepeta*, 73, 84
Callirhoe involucrata, 59
Caltha palustris, 88
Campanula cochleariifolia, 117
Campsis radicans, 38
Caragana arborescens, 102
Centranthus ruber, 70
Ceratoides lanata, 102
Chamaebatiaria millefolium, 102
Chamaecyparis nootkatensis, 79
Chamaemelum nobile, 115
Chelidonium majus, 83
Chrystothamnus nauseosus, 102
Clematis, 20, 59
Cordyline baueri, 23
Cornus alba, 36, 88; *C. stolonifera*, 88
Corydalis ochroleuca, 35
Cotinus coggygria, 19
Cowania mexicana, 103
Crambe maritima, 30, 99
Crocus sativus, 73, 101; *C. spectosus*, 118
Cyclamen hederifolium, 118
Cynara cardunculus, 30; *C. scolymus*, 30
Cytisus, 105

D

Daphne odora, 36; *D. × burkwoodii*, 36
Delosperma sp., 95
Desidilirion wheeleri, 94
Dianthus, 26, 28, 95; *D. caryophyllus*, 29; *D. gratianopolitanus*, 29; *D. plumarius*, 28, 95; *D. × allwoodii*, 29
Digitalis lanata, 100; *D. lutea*, *3*, 35; *D. purpurea*, 80, 100
Doku-dami, 88
Doronicum orientale, 80
Duchesnea indica, 118

E

Echinacea angustifolia, 67; *E. pallida*, 67; *E. purpurea*,

67; *E. tennesseensis*, 67
Echium vulgare, 60
Elymus glaucus, 30
Ephedra nevadensis, 105
Equisetum, 88
Eryngium umbelliferum, 94
Eupatorium capillifolium, 18; *E. coelestinum*, *55*; *E. perfoliatum*, 72; *E. purpureum*, 72

F

Fallugia paradoxa, 103
Felicia bergeriana, 63
Festuca glauca, 30
Fouquieria splendens, 106
Fragaria vesca, 34

G

Galega officinalis, 70
Galium odoratum, 80; *G. vernum*, 16
Geranium cinereum, *14*; *G. maculatum*, 76; *G. platypetalum*, *19*; *G. robertianum*, 74, 80
Gillenia stipulata, 84; *G. trifoliata*, 83
Glaucium flavum, 99
Glycyrrhiza glabra, 30

H

Hedeoma pulegioides, 84
Helianthus annuus, 31
Helichrysum italicum, 29, 106; *H. petiolare*, 18, 30; *splendidum*, 29
Helictotrichon sempervirens, 30
Heracleum mantegazzianum, 78
Heuchera, *9*, 31, *57*, 73
Hosta, 15; *H. sieboldiana*, 80
Houttuynia cordata, 88
Humulus japonicus, 36; *H. lupulus*, 15
Hydrangea, 36
Hypericum calycinum, 83
Hyssopus officinalis, 102

I

Imperata cylindrica, 23
Ipomoea batatas, 16
Iris missouriensis, 88; *I. pallida*, 15, 35; *I. pseudacorus*, 35, 88; *I. versicolor*, 88

J

Juncus, 88
Juniperus chinensis, 105; *J. horizontalis*, 105; *J. squamata*, 105

K

Kerria, 36
Knautia macedonica, 19, *61*

L

Lamium galeobdolon, 80; *L. maculatum*, 117
Laurentia fluviatilis, *109*
Laurus nobilis, 106
Lavandula angustifolia, 69; *L. dentata*, 70; *L. latifolia*, 69; *L. multifida*, 70; *L. stoechas*, 70; *L. × intermedia*, 69
Lavatera trimestris, 63
Leonotis leonurus, 74, 90
Leucophyllum frutescens, 105
Liatris punctata, 100; *L. spicata*, 100
Lilium regale, 36
Linaria purpurea, 100
Lippia dulcis, 126–127
Liriope, 9, 15
Lobelia erinus, 117
Lonicera japonica, 36
Lotus corniculatus, 112
Lunaria annua, 84
Lychnis coronaria, 31
Lysichiton americanum, 88
Lysimachia ciliata, 20

M

Mahonia aquifolium, 79; *M. repens*, 79; *M. rotundifolium*, 18; *M. vulgare*, 18
Mazus reptans, 115
Melissa officinalis, 15, 33
Mentha pulegium, 88; *M. requienii*, 88, 112
Miscanthus sinensis, 35
Monarda citriodora, 20, 48, 69; *M. didyma*, 69; *M. fistulosa*, 69; *M. punctata*, 69
Monardella odoratissima, 105
Myrrhis odorata, 80

N

Nepeta phylloclamys, 29; *N. sibthorpii*, 29; *N. × faassenii*, 29

O

Ocimum, *122*; *O. basilicum*, 20
Onopordum acanthium, 99

Opuntia sp., 106
Origanum laevigatum, 73; *O. vulgare*, 15, 33
Oxypetalum caeruleum, 63

P

Papaver somniferum, 31, 60
Pelargonium, 32, 33
Peltaphyllum peltatum, 86
Pennisetum alopecuroides, 128; *P. setaceum*, 23
Penstemon, 100; *P. strictus*, 95
Pentaglottis sempervirens, 83
Perilla frutescens, 20
Perovskia atriplicifolia, 73, 100
Petrorhagia saxifraga, 95, 112
Phacelia companularia, 95
Phalaris arundinacea, 33, 35
Phlomis alpina, 65, 100
P. cashmeriana, 100; *P. fruticosa*, 100; *P. russeliana*, 100; *P. samia*, 100; *P. tuberosa*, 100
Phormium colensoi, 36; *P. tenax*, 23, 36, 90
Phygelius capensis, 68
Phytolacca americana, 74; *P. clavigera*, 74
Pimpinella anisum, 83
Plantago major, 83
Plectranthus, 63; *P. amboinicus*, 122; *P. argentatus*, 7, 128
Polemonium caeruleum, 83
Polygonum aubertii, 38; *P. aviculare*, 95; *P. bistorta*, 89
Potentilla nevadensis, 112
Primula denticulata, 80; *P. elatior*, 79, 115; *P. veris*, 79, 115; *P. vulgaris*, 79
Prunella grandiflora, 117; *P. laciniata*, 117; *P. vulgaris*, 83; *P. webbiana*, 83
Prunus × cistena, 23
Pulmonaria, *83*, 85

R

Rheum palmatum, 80, 89
Rhus trilobata, 105
Ricinus communis, 23
Rosa canina, 74; *R. gallica*,

74; *R. glauca*, 23, 56; *R. laevigata*, 74; *R. rubiginosa*, 74; *R. rugosa*, 74; *R. sericea*, 24; *R. woodsii*, 105; *R. × harisonii*, 105
Rosmarinus officinalis, 34, 106
Ruta graveolens, 33, 63

S

Sagina subulata, 15, 115
Salix caprea, 88; *S. purpurea*, 88
Salvia argentea, 30, 34, 64; *S. candidissima*, 30; *S. clevelandii*, 30; *S. coccinea*, 128; *S. elegans*, 67; *S. farinacea*, 21; *S. forskaohlei*, 19, 64; *S. frigida*, 30; *S. glutinosa*, 66, *98*; *S. involucrata*, 51, 67; *S. leucantha*, 30, 67, 96; *S. officinalis*, 20, 33–34; *S. patens*, 64; *S. pratensis*, 64, 100; *S. sclarea*, 64, 100
S. viridis, 64, 128
Sambucus nigra, 23, 36
Sanguisorba canadensis, *71*, 71, 72
Santolina chamaecyparissus, 69; *S. rosmarinifolia*, 69
Saponaria ocymoides, 101
Sauromatum venosum, 122
Scabiosa ochroleuca, 35
Sedum 74, 119; *S. acre*, 112; *S. kamtschaticum*, 33, 112; *S. spectabilis*, 26; *S. spurium*, 26, 112
Sempervivum, 117; *S. arachnoideum*, 112
Senecio cineraria, 31, 64; *S. vera-vera*, 24
Silene alpestris, 112; *S. schafta*, 112
Smyrnium perfoliatum, 16
Solanum wrightii, 96
Soleirolia soleirolii, 112
Stachys byzantina, *13*, *14*, 18, 25, 33; *S. grandiflora*, 19, 56; *S. palustris*, 88; *S. sylvatica*, 118
Symphytum grandiflorum, 12, 15; *S. × uplandicum*, 34, 66

T

Tanacetum balsamita var. *tomentosum*, 63; *T. densum* var. *amani*, 70, 73; *T. niveum*, 63; *T. parthenium*, 15, 62; *T. ptarmiciflorum*, 31
Tellima grandiflora, 86
Teucrium scardonicum, 60
Thuja spp., 79
Thymus, 111; *T. praecox* subsp. *arcticus*, 111; *T. vulgaris*, 111; *T. × citriodorus*, 34, 111
Tiboucina, 128–129
Tovara virginica, *57*
Tribulus terrestris, 95
Trillium sessile, 80
Tulbaghia violacea, 35, 101
Tulipa greigii, 20

U

Umbellularia californica, 106

V

Valeriana officinalis, 70; *V. phu*, 12, 80
Verbascum blattaria, 99; *V. bombyciferum*, 31, *98*, 98, 99; *V. chaixii*, 99; *V. thapsus*, 99; *V. widemannianum*, 99
Verbena hastata, 89; *V. officinalis*, 70; *V. patagonica*, 22–23, *51*, 59
Veronica cinerea, 29; *V. filiformis*, 108; *V. incana*, 29; *V. liwanensis*, 112; *V. pectinata*, 112
Viburnum × burkwoodii, 79
Viola corsica, 117; *V. labradorica*, 117; *V. tricolor*, 117
Virbunum × rhytidophylloides, 79

W

Weigela, 36

Y

Yucca filamentosa, *13*, 35, 62, 106; *Y. glauca*, 106